THE LEGAL SYSTEM AND SERVICES OF ENGLAND AND WALES

For 2027 exams

Amy Sixsmith

Series editors: Amy Sixsmith and David Sixsmith

REVISE SQE

First edition published in 2021 by Fink Publishing Ltd
This edition published in 2026

Impression number 10 9 8 7 6 5 4 3 2 1

British Library Cataloguing in Publication Data
A catalogue record for this book is available from the British Library
ISBN: 9781807730000

This book is also available in various ebook formats.
Ebook ISBN: 9781807730024

Production and typesetting by Westchester Publishing Services (UK)
Cover and text design by BMLD (bmld.uk)
Multiple-choice questions advisor: Mark Thomas

Fink Publishing Ltd
E-mail: hello@finkpublishing.com
www.revise4law.co.uk

Notes from the publisher

1. This book reflects the SQE1 assessment specification (updated April 2026) applicable for assessments from 1 September 2026.

2. While Fink Publishing has made every attempt to ensure that advice on the qualification and its assessment is accurate, the official specification and associated assessment guidance materials are the only authoritative source of information and should always be referred to for definitive guidance. See the SRA website at https://sqe.sra.org.uk. Note that the SRA may amend their assessment guidance (including the contents of the assessment specifications) at any point.

3. Fink Publishing has robust editorial processes to ensure the accuracy of the content in this publication, and every effort is made to ensure this publication is free of errors. We are, however, only human, and occasionally errors do occur. Fink Publishing is not liable for any misunderstandings that arise as a result of errors in this publication, but it is our priority to ensure that the content is accurate. If you spot an error, please do contact us at revise4law.co.uk so we can make sure it is corrected.

Contents

Contributors

THE AUTHOR

Dr Amy Sixsmith is associate professor in law at the University of Sunderland. She has taught law to undergraduate and postgraduate students for over 16 years and has extensive experience of helping law students to develop a wide range of legal skills.

SERIES EDITORS

Dr Amy Sixsmith is also an editor for this series.

Dr David Sixsmith is assistant professor in law at Northumbria Law School and a senior fellow of Advance HE.

Introduction to Revise SQE

Welcome to *Revise SQE*, a series of revision guides designed to help you in your preparation for, and achievement in, the Solicitors Qualifying Examination 1 (SQE1) assessment. SQE1 is designed to assess what the Solicitors Regulation Authority (SRA) refer to as 'functioning legal knowledge' (FLK); this is the legal knowledge and competencies required of a newly qualified solicitor in England and Wales. The SRA has chosen single best answer multiple-choice questions (MCQs) to test this knowledge, and *Revise SQE* is here to help.

PREPARING YOURSELF FOR SQE

The SQE is the relatively new route to qualification for aspiring solicitors, introduced in September 2021 as one of the final stages towards qualification as a solicitor. The SQE consists of two parts:

SQE1

- **Functioning legal knowledge (FLK)**
  - two x 180 MCQs
  - closed book; assessed by two sittings, over 10 hours in total

SQE2

- **Practical legal skills**
  - 16 written and oral assessments
  - assesses six practical legal skills over 14 hours in total

In addition to the above, any candidate will have to undertake two years' qualifying work experience. More information on the SQE assessments can be found on the SRA's dedicated SQE website; this revision guide series will focus on FLK and preparation for SQE1.

It is important to note that the SQE can be perceived to be a 'harder' set of assessments than the Legal Practice Course (LPC). The reason for this, explained by the SRA, is that the LPC is designed to prepare candidates for 'day one' of their training contract; the SQE, on the other hand, is designed to prepare candidates for 'day one' of being a newly qualified solicitor. Indeed, the SRA has chosen the SQE1 assessment to be 'closed book' (ie without permitting use of any materials) on the basis that a newly qualified solicitor would know all of the information tested, without having to refer to books or other sources.

With that in mind, and a different style of assessments in place, it is understandable that many readers may feel nervous or wary of the SQE. This is especially so given that this style of assessment is likely to be different from what readers will have experienced before. In this *Introduction* and revision guide series, we hope to alleviate some of those concerns with guidance on preparing for the SQE assessment, tips on how to approach single best answer MCQs and expertly written guides to aid in your revision.

What does SQE1 entail?

SQE1 consists of two assessments, containing 180 single best answer MCQs each (360 MCQs in total). The table below breaks down what is featured in each of these assessments.

Assessment	Contents of assessment ('functioning legal knowledge')
FLK assessment 1	• Business law and practice • Dispute resolution • Contract • Tort • The legal system (the legal system of England and Wales and sources of law, constitutional and administrative law and European Union law and legal services)
FLK assessment 2	• Property practice • Wills and the administration of estates • Solicitors accounts • Land law • Trusts • Criminal law and practice

Please be aware that in addition to the above, ethics and professional conduct will be examined pervasively across the two assessments (ie it could crop up anywhere).

Each substantive topic is allocated a percentage of the assessment paper (eg 'legal services' will form 12–16% of the FLK1 assessment) and is broken down further into 'core principles'. Candidates are advised to read the SQE1 Assessment Specification in full (available on the SQE website). We have also provided a *Revise SQE checklist* to help you in your preparation and revision for SQE1 (see below).

HOW DO I PREPARE FOR SQE1?

Given the vastly different nature of SQE1 compared to anything you may have done previously, it can be quite daunting to consider how you could possibly prepare for 360 single best answer MCQs, spanning 11 different substantive topics (especially given that it is 'closed book'). The *Revise SQE FAQ* below, however, will set you off on the right path to success.

Revise SQE FAQ

Question	Answer
1. Where do I start?	We would advise that you begin by reviewing the assessment specification for SQE1. You need to identify what subject matter can be assessed under each substantive topic. For each topic, you should honestly ask yourself whether you would be prepared to answer an MCQ on that topic in SQE1. We have helped you in this process by providing a *Revise SQE checklist* on our website (revise4law.co.uk) that allows you to read the subject matter of each topic and identify where you consider your knowledge to be at any given time. We have also helpfully cross-referenced each topic to a chapter and page of our *Revise SQE* revision guides.
2. Do I need to know legal authorities, such as case law?	In the majority of circumstances, candidates are not required to know or use legal authorities. This includes statutory provisions, case law or procedural rules. Of course, candidates will need to be aware of legal principles deriving from common law and statute. There may be occasions, however, where the assessment specification does identify a legal authority (such as *Rylands v Fletcher* in tort law). In this case, candidates will be required to know the name of that case, the principles of that case and how to apply that case to the facts of an MCQ. These circumstances are clearly highlighted in the assessment specification and candidates are advised to ensure they engage with those legal authorities in full. In each of our texts in the Revise SQE series, we detail clearly which authorities are required for that subject. Any authorities provided in addition are designed to assist in your revision by acting as an aide-mémoire.
3. Do I need to know the history behind a certain area of law?	While understanding the history and development of a certain area of law is beneficial, there is no requirement for you to know or prepare for any questions relating to the development of the law (eg in criminal law,

Revise SQE FAQ (continued)

Question	Answer
	candidates will not need to be aware of the development from objective to subjective recklessness). SQE1 will be testing a candidate's knowledge of the law as it stands four calendar months prior to the date of the first assessment in an assessment window. The SRA on the SQE website has helpfully provided the exact cut-off date for each assessment in the cycle; it is worth checking this when you are preparing for your assessment.
4. Do I need to be aware of academic opinion or proposed reforms to the law?	Candidates preparing for SQE1 do not need to focus on critical evaluation of the law, or proposed reforms to the law either.
5. How do I prepare for single best answer MCQs?	See our separate *Revise SQE* guide on preparing for single best answer MCQs below.

Where does *Revise SQE* come into it?

The *Revise SQE* series of revision guides is designed to aid your revision and consolidate your understanding; the series is not designed to replace your substantive learning of the SQE1 topics. We hope that this series will provide clarity as to assessment focus, useful tips for sitting SQE1 and act as a general revision aid.

There are also materials on our website to help you prepare and revise for the SQE1, such as a *Revise SQE checklist*. This *checklist* is designed to help you identify which substantive topics you feel confident about heading into the exam - see below for an example.

Revise SQE checklist

The Legal System and Services of England and Wales

SQE content	Corresponding chapter	***Revise SQE checklist***		
The courts • The judiciary	Chapter 1, page 3	I do not know this subject and I am not ready for SQE1 ☐	I partially know this subject, but I am not ready for SQE1 ☐	I know this subject and I am ready for SQE1 ☐

The Legal System and Services of England and Wales (continued)

SQE content	Corresponding chapter	*Revise SQE checklist*		
The courts • Court hierarchy, the appeal system and jurisdiction	Chapter 1, pages 9–20	I do not know this subject and I am not ready for SQE1 ☐	I partially know this subject, but I am not ready for SQE1 ☐	I know this subject and I am ready for SQE1 ☐
The courts • Rights of audience	Chapter 1, pages 20–22	I do not know this subject and I am not ready for SQE1 ☐	I partially know this subject, but I am not ready for SQE1 ☐	I know this subject and I am ready for SQE1 ☐

PREPARING FOR SINGLE BEST ANSWER MCQS

As discussed above, SQE1 will be a challenging assessment for all candidates. This is partly due to the quantity of information a candidate must be aware of in two separate sittings. In addition, however, an extra complexity is added due to the nature of the assessment itself: MCQs.

The SRA has identified that MCQs are the most appropriate way to test a candidate's knowledge and understanding of fundamental legal principles. While this may be the case, it is likely that many candidates have little, if any, experience of MCQs as part of their previous study. Even if a candidate does have experience of MCQs, SQE1 will feature a special form of MCQs known as 'single best answer' questions.

What are single best answer MCQs and what do they look like?

Single best answer MCQs are a specialised form of question, used extensively in other fields such as in training medical professionals. The idea behind single best answer MCQs is that the multitude of options available to a candidate may each bear merit, sharing commonalities and correct statements of law or principle, but only one option is absolutely correct (in the sense that it is the 'best' answer). In this regard, single best answer MCQs are different from traditional MCQs.

A traditional MCQ will feature answers that are implausible in the sense that the distractors are 'obviously wrong'. Indeed, distractors in a traditional MCQ are often very dissimilar, resulting in a candidate being able to spot answers that are clearly wrong with greater ease.

In a well-constructed single best answer MCQ, on the other hand, each option should look equally attractive given their similarities and subtle differences. The skill of the candidate will be identifying which, out of the options provided, is the single best answer. This requires a much greater level of engagement with the question than a traditional MCQ would require; candidates must take the time to read the questions carefully in the exam.

How are single best answer MCQs structured?

For SQE1, single best answer MCQs will be structured as follows:

A woman is charged with battery, having thrown a rock towards another person intending to scare them. The rock hits the person in the head, causing no injury. The woman claims that she never intended that the rock hit the person, but the prosecution allege that the woman was reckless as to whether the rock would hit the other person.	**The factual scenario.** First, the candidate will be provided with a factual scenario that sets the scene for the question to be asked (known as the 'stem').
Which of the following is the most accurate statement regarding the test for recklessness in relation to a battery?	**The lead in.** Next, the candidate will be provided with the question that they must find the single best answer to.
A. There must have been a risk that force would be applied by the rock, and that the reasonable person would have foreseen that risk and unjustifiably taken it. B. There must have been a risk that force would be applied by the rock, and that the woman should have foreseen that risk and unjustifiably taken it. C. There must have been a risk that force would be applied by the rock, and that the woman must have foreseen that risk and unjustifiably taken it. D. There must have been a risk that force would be applied by the rock, and that both the woman and the reasonable person should have foreseen that risk and unjustifiably taken it. E. There must have been a risk that force would be applied by the rock, but there is no requirement that the risk be foreseen.	**The possible answers.** Finally, the candidate will be provided with **five** possible answers. There is only one single best answer that must be chosen. The other answers, known as 'distractors', are not the 'best' answer available.

It will be beneficial to guide you through each aspect of the MCQ to further your understanding of the writing process.

The stem

The stem (ie scenario) will differ according to each MCQ and what it is seeking to test. If the MCQ is seeking simply to test a candidate's basic knowledge of the law, without application, then the stem is likely to be short. Where, however, the MCQ is seeking to have a candidate analyse a factual pattern, and apply it to the options available, the stem will be significantly longer.

In general, however, a stem should be a concise and clear introduction to the issue at hand. A well written stem should contain all material facts relevant to answering the question about to be asked (new facts should not be introduced in the lead in or the distractors). The stem should not be ambiguous or open to interpretation.

The lead in

The lead in will be a short question and can be phrased in a variety of ways. The lead in should provide the candidate with everything they need to answer the question. There should be no ambiguity or double meanings.

The length and nature of the lead in will vary dependent on the type of question being asked. These categories of MCQ are detailed in the table below.

Categories of MCQs	Explanation and example
'Knows' MCQs	To *recall* a specific answer (eg the author of X is Y)
'Shows How' MCQs	To *analyse* a fact pattern and *apply* (eg the application of X in this case is Y)
'Knows How' MCQs	To *know* the answer, and *show* the reason *why* (eg the purpose of X is Y because ...)

Most commonly, a lead in may be phrased as:
- Which of the following statements best describes ...?
- Which of the following statements best summarises ...?
- Which of the following best explains ...?

A lead in will not, however, be phrased as:
- Which of the following is true?
- What is the rule for X?
- Which one of the following is not correct?

The options

You will be provided with five possible answers and only one is correct (whether that be outright correct, or the single best).

The options will not ask a candidate to identify multiple options as being correct (eg 'A, C and D are correct; B and E are wrong'). Nor will the options feature an 'all of the above' option.

A well written MCQ will avoid vague language in the options. Words such as 'rarely', 'usually' etc should be avoided as they present too much ambiguity. On the other hand, absolute words such as 'only', 'always' and 'never' should equally be avoided because they are often obvious distractors (there rarely being a circumstance in English and Welsh law where the legal position is absolute without exception).

If written well, each option should be plausible (meaning that some candidates would choose it). Plausibility can come from drawing on faulty reasoning and common misconceptions. It may be the case that some options share identical wording save for one word (eg a change from 'may' to 'must'). You therefore need to pay close attention to the wording of the options.

To achieve that, all options will be of a fairly equal length to ensure that they are consistent with one another. It is often said that the correct answer is likely to be the longest; so the writers of the MCQs will have that in mind.

In addition, to ensure plausibility, each option is either likely to be a variation of the other, or each option will be entirely different to the others. MCQ drafters will often rely on the rule of 'Three and Two'. The idea behind this rule is that three options will be fairly similar to each other (eg starting with 'Yes'), whilst the remaining two answers will be equally similar to each other (eg starting with 'No'). If you know the answer is definitely 'Yes', that therefore removes the 'No' options immediately. If the MCQ has not adopted the rule of Three and Two, it is likely that you will be able to pick out the 'obvious' distractor.

Now that you know what the MCQs will look like on SQE1, let us talk about how you may go about tackling an MCQ.

How do I tackle single best answer MCQs?

No exact art exists in terms of answering single best answer MCQs; your success depends on your subject knowledge and understanding of how that subject knowledge can be applied. Despite this, there are tips and tricks that may be helpful for you to consider when confronted with a single best answer MCQ.

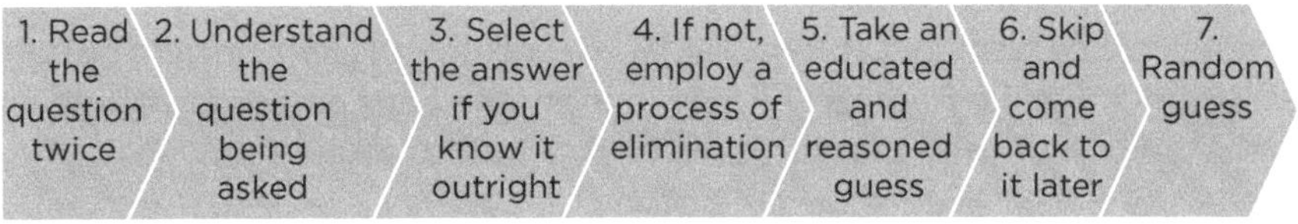

These tips and tricks are essential for preparing you to sit the SQE1 assessment. Each session will involve 90 MCQs, to be answered over 2 hours, 33 minutes. Answering 90 MCQs in that timescale allows *1 minute, 42 seconds per question,* under exam conditions. Of course, some questions will take more or less time to answer than others.

Please take a moment to think about that: on average, within 1 minute and 42 seconds you will have to:

- read the MCQ, including the various answers
- distil from that MCQ what the question is assessing
- work out which of the five possible answers is the correct (or 'single best') answer.

This will be an intensive assessment. You must ensure that you are properly prepared for it, in terms of your subject knowledge and also your mental resilience and time management. Your ability to navigate MCQs will also assist greatly.

1. Read the entire question at least twice

This sounds obvious but is so often overlooked. You are advised to read the entire question once, taking in all relevant pieces of information, understanding what the question is asking you and being aware of the options available. Once you have done that, read the entire question again and this time pay careful attention to the wording that is used.

- **In the factual scenario:** Does it use any words that stand out? Do any words used have legal bearing? What are you told and what are you not told?
- **In the lead in:** What are you being asked? Are there certain words to look out for (eg 'should', 'must', 'will', 'shall')?
- **In the answers:** What are the differences between each option? Are they substantial differences or subtle differences? Do any differences turn on a word or a phrase?

You should be prepared to give each question at least two viewings to mitigate any misunderstandings or oversights.

2. Understand the question being asked

It is important first that you understand what the question is asking of you. The SRA has identified that the FLK assessments may consist of single best answer MCQs that, for example:

- require the candidate to simply identify a correct legal principle or rule;
- require the candidate to not only identify the correct legal principle or rule, but also apply that principle or rule to the factual scenario;
- provide the candidate with the correct legal principle or rule, but require the candidate to identify how it should be properly applied and/or the outcome of that proper application.

By first identifying what the question is asking you to do, you can then understand what the creators of that question are seeking to test and how to approach the answers available. Many candidates actually find it beneficial to start with the lead in, before reading the scenario. This gives them the opportunity to understand what the scenario will likely entail. You need to decide what works best for you, so take the opportunity to try both ways.

3. Select the answer if you know it outright

You may feel as though a particular answer 'jumps out' at you, and that you are certain it is correct. It is very likely that the answer is correct. While you should be confident in your answers, do not allow your confidence (and perhaps overconfidence) to rush you into making a decision. Review all of your options one final time before you move on to the next question.

4. If you do not know the answer outright, employ a process of elimination

There may be situations in which the answer is not obvious from the outset. This may be due to the close similarities between different answers. Remember, it is the 'single best answer' that you are looking for. If you keep this in your mind, it will thereafter be easier to employ a process of elimination. Identify which answers you are sure are not correct (or not the 'best') and whittle down your options. Get rid of the distractors. Once you have only two options remaining, carefully scrutinise the wording used in both answers and look back to the question being asked. Identify what you consider to the be the best answer, in light of that question. Review your answer and move on to the next question.

5. Take an educated and reasoned guess

There may be circumstances, quite commonly, in which you do not know the answer to the question. In this circumstance, you should try as hard as possible to eliminate any distractors that you are positive are incorrect and then take an educated and reasoned guess based on the options available. 'Always select C' will not work in this assessment; the correct answers will be randomly distributed amongst the MCQs as options A–E.

6. Skip and come back to it later

If time permits, you may think it appropriate to skip a question that you are unsure of and return to it before the end of the assessment. The assessment portal will highlight any questions that have not been answered, and you are also able to 'flag' questions for your review later on in the assessment (time permitting). If you do so, we would advise that you:

- make a note of what question you have skipped or click 'Flag for Review' on your screen, and
- ensure you leave sufficient time for you to go back to that question before the end of the assessment.

The same advice is applicable to any question that you have answered but for which you remain unsure.

7. Random guess

As a matter of absolute last resort, being unable even to take an educated and reasoned guess, you should simply choose an answer. There is no negative marking in the SQE1 assessments, so it is better for you to select an answer with the possibility, by sheer luck, of answering it correctly than it is to leave the answer blank and have no chance of scoring a point. The advice is simple: answer all of the questions, even if you have to guess at the end.

We hope that this brief guide will assist you in your preparation towards, and engagement with, single best answer MCQs.

GUIDED TOUR

Each chapter contains a number of features to help you revise, apply and test your knowledge.

Make sure you know Each chapter begins with an overview of the main topics covered and why you need to understand them for the purpose of the SQE1 assessments.

SQE assessment advice This identifies what you need to pay particular attention to in your revision as you work through the chapter.

What do you know already? These questions help you to assess which topics you feel confident with and which topics you may need to spend more time on (and where to find them in the chapter).

Key term Key terms are highlighted in bold where they first appear and defined in a separate box.

Exam warning This feature offers advice on where it is possible to go wrong in the assessments.

Revision tip Throughout the chapters are ideas to help you revise effectively and be best prepared for the assessment.

Summary This handy box brings together key information in an easy to revise and remember form.

Practice example These examples take a similar format to SQE-type questions and provide an opportunity to see how content might be applied to a scenario.

Procedural link Where relevant, this element shows how a concept might apply to another procedural topic in the series.

Key point checklist At the end of each chapter there is a bullet-point summary of its most important content.

Key terms and concepts These are listed at the end of each chapter to help ensure you know, or can revise, terms and concepts you will need to be familiar with for the assessments.

SQE-style questions Five SQE-style questions on the chapter topic give you an opportunity to test your knowledge.

Answers to questions Check how you did with answers to both the quick knowledge test from the start of the chapter and the SQE-style questions at the end of the chapter.

Key cases, rules, statutes and instruments These list the key sources candidates need to be familiar with for the SQE assessment.

SQE1 TABLE OF LEGAL AUTHORITIES

The SQE1 Assessment Specification states the following in respect of legal authorities and their relevance to SQE1:

> On occasion in legal practice a case name or statutory provision, for example, is the term normally used to describe a legal principle or an area of law, or a rule or procedural step (eg *Rylands v Fletcher*, CPR Part 36, Section 25 notice). In such circumstances, candidates are required to know and be able to use such case names, statutory provisions etc. In all other circumstances candidates are not required to recall specific case names, or cite statutory or regulatory authorities.

This *SQE1 table of legal authorities* identifies the legal authorities you are required to know for the purpose of the SQE1 Functioning Legal Knowledge assessments for *The Legal System of England and Wales and Sources of Law and Legal Services.*

Legal authority	Corresponding *Revise SQE* chapter/pages
Equality Act 2010	**Chapter 6: Overriding legal obligations, page 110**
Proceeds of Crime Act 2002	**Chapter 6: Overriding legal obligations, page 124**
Financial Services and Markets Act 2000 and 'related secondary legislation'	**Chapter 7: Financial services, page 139**
• Financial Services and Markets Act 2000 (Regulated Activities) Order 2001, SI 2001/544	**Chapter 7: Financial services, page 140**
• Financial Services and Markets Act 2000 (Professions) (Non-Exempt Activities) Order 2001, SI 2001/1227	**Chapter 7: Financial services, page 149**
• Financial Services and Markets Act 2000 (Financial Promotion) Order 2005, SI 2005/1529	**Chapter 7: Financial services, page 148**
• SRA Financial Services (Scope) Rules 2001	**Chapter 7: Financial services, page 146**
• SRA Financial Services (Conduct of Business) Rules 2001	**Chapter 7: Financial services, page 147**

TABLE OF CASES

TABLE OF STATUTES

1

The court structure of England and Wales

■ MAKE SURE YOU KNOW

This chapter provides an overview of the court hierarchy of England and Wales and examines the role and jurisdiction of the various courts that make up the English legal system. For the SQE1 assessments you will need to understand the function and jurisdiction of each court within the court structure. You will also need to understand the judicial hierarchy, and the rules governing the exercise of rights of audience. Your understanding of these subjects will enable you to identify and apply the appropriate legal rules and principles to realistic client-based scenarios in the SQE assessments.

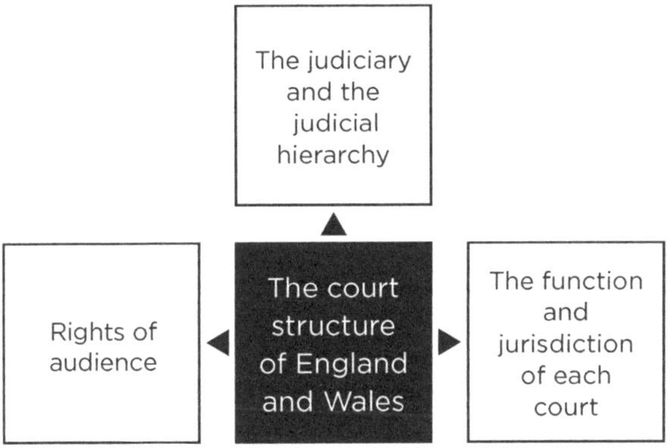

■ SQE ASSESSMENT ADVICE

The questions that you are required to answer in the SQE1 assessments are designed to test your ability to identify and apply fundamental legal principles to realistic client-based and ethical problems and situations. In order to prepare for the FLK1 assessment, you will need to ensure that you know and understand the key legal principles underpinning the operation of the legal system of England and Wales. You must, however, also ensure that you are able to correctly *apply* that knowledge to realistic client-based problem scenarios. For example, a question may require you to determine which court(s) or judge(s) have the power to hear a client's matter. The important point to note is that the FLK1 assessment requires you to demonstrate a *practical* understanding of the court structure of England and Wales.

The SQE1 Assessment Specification, which can be accessed via the SRA's website, states that the FLK1 assessment may test your knowledge and understanding of various courts which make up the legal system of England and Wales.

As you work through this chapter, make sure that you pay particular attention to the following topics:

- the judicial hierarchy
- the function and jurisdiction of each court within the legal system
- the rules surrounding the acquisition and exercise of rights of audience.

■ WHAT DO YOU KNOW ALREADY?

Have a go at these questions before reading this chapter. If you find some difficult or cannot remember the answers, make a note to look more closely at that topic in your revision.

1) What does the term 'jurisdiction' mean in the context of the English legal system?

   [Jurisdiction: overview, page 5]

2) True or false: The burden of proof refers to the degree to which a party must prove their case.

   [Jurisdiction: overview, page 5]

3) Which of the following statements is most accurate?

   a) The magistrates' court deals with all summary offences and triable either way offences.

   b) The magistrates' court deals with summary offences and some triable either way offences.

   c) The magistrates' court deals with summary offences, triable either way offences and less serious indictable offences.

   [Jurisdiction and role of each court in the court structure of England and Wales, page 10]

4) What is meant by the term 'judicial hierarchy' and how does this differ from 'court hierarchy'?

   [The judicial hierarchy, page 3]

5) True or false: solicitors are automatically granted higher rights of

audience and can use these powers once they are admitted or registered to the roll of solicitors.

[Rights of audience, page 20]

THE JUDICIAL HIERARCHY

The SQE FLK1 assessment requires you to demonstrate that you understand how the English legal system operates. An area you will need to understand is the role that judges play in the administration of justice. Collectively the various judges who preside over cases constitute the **judiciary** of England and Wales.

Key term: judiciary

The term 'judiciary' refers to the various types of judges that work within the English legal system.

It is important to understand that there is a **judicial hierarchy**. In basic terms, this means that some judges have greater powers and responsibilities than others. Unsurprisingly, the judges at the top of the judicial hierarchy have more extensive powers and responsibilities than those lower in the hierarchy. Judges tend to sit in the courts that correspond with their position in the judicial hierarchy. There are a number of 'senior' judges defined by statute (Constitutional Reform Act (CRA) 2005, s 60(1)). These senior judicial posts encompass both judicial *and* important administrative roles. Technically, all other judges are 'inferior'. Nevertheless, some inferior judges are more powerful than others and so are 'higher' in the judicial hierarchy. They are considered to be more powerful because the powers they can exercise are not limited by statute. Other inferior judges have powers that have been specifically defined by statute.

Key term: judicial hierarchy

The judicial hierarchy ranks the various members of the judiciary by virtue of the powers and responsibilities associated with each judicial office/post.

You will need a good understanding of the judicial hierarchy to properly understand the court hierarchy, discussed later in this chapter.

Revision tip

Your understanding of the judicial hierarchy will also help you to understand the appeals process. In SQE1, the civil appeals process is assessed as part of dispute resolution; you can revise this topic by reading ***Revise SQE: Dispute Resolution*, Chapter 11**. The criminal appeals process is assessed as part of criminal practice; you can revise this topic by reading ***Revise SQE: Criminal Practice*, Chapter 9**.

Table 1.1: The judicial hierarchy

Judicial office	Typical court	Status in judicial hierarchy
Lord Chief Justice	Court of Appeal	Senior judicial office
President of the Supreme Court	Supreme Court and Privy Council	Senior judicial office
Master of the Rolls	Court of Appeal	Senior judicial office
Justice of the Supreme Court	Supreme Court and Privy Council	Senior judicial office
President of the King's Bench Division/Chancery Division/Family Division	High Court	Judicial powers not restricted by statute
Lord Justices of Appeal	Court of Appeal	Judicial powers not restricted by statute
High Court judge	High Court, Crown Court, Family Court	Judicial powers not restricted by statute
Circuit judge	County Court, Crown Court, Family Court	Judicial powers restricted by statute
Recorder	County Court, Crown Court, Family Court	Judicial powers restricted by statute
District judge	County Court, High Court, Family Court	Judicial powers restricted by statute
District judge (magistrates' court)	magistrates' court, Family Court	Judicial powers restricted by statute

You should use **Table 1.1** (above) to learn which judges typically sit in which courts, and where each type of judge 'sits' in the judicial hierarchy. We will then examine the concept of **jurisdiction** in detail.

JURISDICTION: OVERVIEW

Jurisdiction refers to the power that a court or a judge has to consider different types of cases.

Key term: jurisdiction
Jurisdiction refers to the power that a court or judge has to hear a case.

The term jurisdiction may refer to the *type* of law that the court typically deals with. For example, it is common to refer to courts as being either *criminal* courts or *civil* courts. The key differences between civil and criminal cases are briefly outlined below.

Distinguishing between civil and criminal cases

Criminal cases are cases where a prosecution has been brought against an individual (referred to as a *defendant*) who is believed to have committed a criminal offence. Prosecutions are typically brought against individuals by the Crown Prosecution Service (CPS) on behalf of the state (referred to as the *prosecution*). The core function of criminal courts is to determine the guilt or innocence of a defendant. If a defendant is found guilty of an offence, the court must also determine an appropriate sentence for the defendant.

Civil cases, on the other hand, primarily involve the resolution of private disputes between individuals. Typically, the person bringing the claim (referred to as the *claimant*) is seeking some sort of legal remedy. The other party to a civil case is usually referred to as *the defendant*. For example, Amy and Barry entered into a contractual agreement for the sale of a car. Amy believes that Barry has breached a term of their contract. Amy may bring a civil action against Barry. The purpose of the case would be to determine whether Barry has breached the term of the contract, and if he has, to determine an appropriate legal remedy for Amy.

The degree to which a party needs to prove their case varies depending on whether the case is a civil case or a criminal case. This is known as the **standard of proof**.

- In criminal cases the standard of proof *is beyond a reasonable doubt*. This is a high threshold to meet.

- In civil cases, the standard of proof is on *the balance of probabilities*. The standard of proof in a civil case is lower than in criminal cases.

The party who bears the responsibility for proving a civil claim must be able to show that what they claim to have occurred is *more likely than not true*.

Key term: standard of proof

The term 'standard of proof' refers to the degree to which a party must prove their case in order to succeed.

The party who bears the responsibility for proving a case is different in civil and criminal cases. The term **burden of proof** is used to identify which party to a case is responsible for proving the case. Generally, in a civil case the *claimant* bears responsibility for proving the case. The burden of proof rests with the claimant. In the example above, Amy is the claimant so she would need to prove, on the balance of probabilities, that Barry breached the term of the contract. In a criminal case, the burden of proof generally rests with the *prosecution*. This means that it is for the prosecution to prove that the defendant committed the offence; it is not for the defendant to prove their innocence.

Key term: burden of proof

The term 'burden of proof' refers to the party who bears responsibility for proving the case.

Table 1.2 summarises the key features of civil and criminal cases. When you revise this topic for the SQE, ensure you can:
- identify whether a case is a civil or criminal matter
- identify the relevant standard of proof
- identify who the relevant burden of proof rests with.

Table 1.2: The key differences between criminal and civil cases

	Criminal	Civil
Parties to a case	Prosecution and defence	Claimant and defendant
Key purpose of the case	Determine guilt or innocence of defendant Determine appropriate sentence	Resolution of legal dispute Determine appropriate legal remedy
Burden of proof	Rests with prosecution	Rests with claimant

Table 1.2: Continued

	Criminal	Civil
Standard of proof	Beyond a reasonable doubt	On the balance of probabilities
Worked example	The CPS believe they have sufficient evidence to prove, beyond all reasonable doubt, that Cyril committed theft. Theft is a criminal offence contrary to the Theft Act 1968. The CPS may bring a prosecution against Cyril.	Duncan trips over an uneven paving slab on a public road. He falls and suffers various injuries and has to take time off work. Duncan may bring an action against the person/body responsible for the maintenance and upkeep of the pavement. Duncan may seek damages to compensate him for the pain and suffering he has endured and for lost earnings.

Practice example 1.1 gives you an example of how this topic might be assessed in the SQE assessment.

Practice example 1.1

A case concerning a very complex commercial contract dispute has commenced in the High Court. The claimant and defendant disagree about whether a term has been incorporated into a contract. The claimant alleges that the parties verbally agreed to incorporate the term into their contract. The defendant alleges that no such verbal agreement was reached and, as such, the claimant cannot rely on the term in question.

What is the relevant standard of proof in this case, and with whom does the burden of proof rest?

This case concerns a contract law dispute and is therefore a civil case. The standard of proof is the balance of probabilities. The burden of proof rests with the claimant.

You should now understand the key features of both civil and criminal cases. Remember that some courts deal predominately with either civil or criminal cases and are therefore described as having civil or criminal jurisdiction (this is explored further on **page 10**). Cases can also be categorised as cases of first instance *or* appeal cases:

- Courts that hear cases at first instance are said to have *trial jurisdiction*.
- Courts that hear appeals are described as having *appellate jurisdiction*.

Trial and appellate jurisdiction

The key differences between trial and appellate cases are summarised as follows:

- When a case is considered for the first time, it is heard in a *court of first instance*.
- *All* cases will *always* commence in a court of first instance.
- If a court usually hears cases in the first instance, it is referred to as a 'court of first instance' or a 'trial court'. The key function of these courts is to determine the facts of the case and to reach a decision on how the relevant law ought to apply to those facts.
- If any party to a case disagrees with how the law has been interpreted or applied, they may be able to *appeal* the decision of the court of first instance.
- Appeals are considered by *appellate* courts. If a court has jurisdiction to hear appeal cases, it is referred to as having 'appellate jurisdiction'. The appellate courts consider questions of *law*, rather than questions of *fact*.

Finally, you should also be aware that some courts are described as 'senior' courts under the Senior Courts Act 1981. Unless a court is classified as a senior court, it has limited powers and is subject to review by senior courts. Section 1 classifies the following courts as 'senior' courts:

- Crown Court
- High Court
- Court of Appeal.

The Supreme Court is, by virtue of s 40 of the CRA 2005, a superior court of record and is the highest court in the English legal system. Put simply, the decisions of senior courts may be subject to review by the Supreme Court because it is the *final* court of appeal for civil and criminal cases in England and Wales.

A good understanding of jurisdiction is essential because it underpins your understanding of the court structure, the appeals process and precedent. Furthermore, in the SQE FLK1 assessment, you may be required to analyse a client-based scenario and *correctly* identify or determine the following:

- whether it is a civil or criminal matter
- whether it is a trial case or an appeal case
- the statement which most accurately describes the nature of such cases
- the applicable standard of proof

- the party that bears the burden of proof
- whether the court concerned is classified as a senior court and what this means.

To be able to identify the relevant court(s) that hear different types of cases, you need to ensure that you have a good knowledge and understanding of the court structure and the jurisdiction and function of each court within the court structure. These topics are explored in the sections that follow.

THE COURT STRUCTURE OF ENGLAND AND WALES

The court system is made up of various courts and each has a distinct role to play in the administration of justice. There is a **court hierarchy**, and this determines which courts bind or influence the decisions made by other courts in the hierarchy. When revising for the SQE FLK1 assessment, it is important that you know the role that each court plays and understand the relationships between different courts. A good understanding of court hierarchy is *essential* to understanding the concept of judicial precedent, which is examined in detail in **Chapter 4**.

Key term: court hierarchy

The court hierarchy establishes which decisions must be followed by other courts in the system. Generally speaking, the higher up a court is in the hierarchy, the more authoritative its decisions.

Figure 1.1 illustrates the overarching court structure. It will be useful to refer back to this diagram as you work through the overview of each

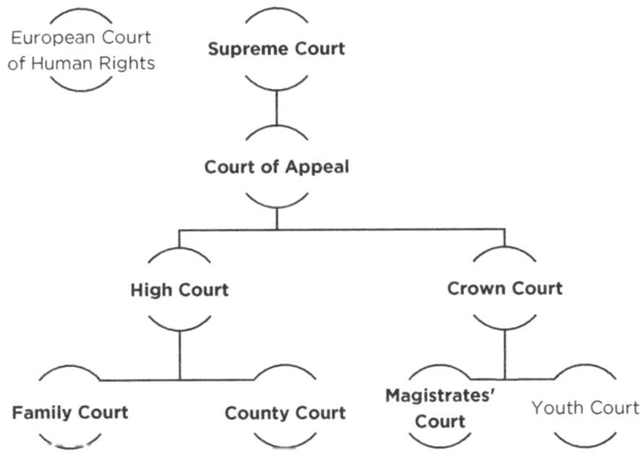

Figure 1.1: The court system

court in the court system. The section that follows provides a concise overview of the function and jurisdiction of each court in the English legal system.

JURISDICTION AND ROLE OF EACH COURT IN THE COURT STRUCTURE OF ENGLAND AND WALES

In the SQE1 assessments, it is probable that you will be required to analyse a client-based scenario and correctly identify which court(s) has the authority to hear the case. You should use this section of the book to revise the key features of each court in the English legal system and make sure that you understand the role and jurisdiction of the various courts which make up the English legal system.

Supreme Court

Apart from cases concerning the European Convention on Human Rights, the Supreme Court is the highest appeal court on civil and criminal matters in the UK. The European Court of Human Rights has jurisdiction for cases involving the interpretation or application of the European Convention on Human Rights.

The Supreme Court only hears appeal cases involving a point of law that is of public importance. It has appellate jurisdiction *only*. No cases, no matter how important, can start in the Supreme Court.

Court of Appeal

The Court of Appeal is split into two divisions: the Civil Division and the Criminal Division. The Civil Division hears appeals on civil matters and the Criminal Division hears appeals on criminal matters. Like the Supreme Court, the Court of Appeal *only* hears appeal cases. It will only hear cases that involve a question of law.

High Court

The High Court is comprised of three distinct divisions:

- the King's Bench Division
- the Chancery Division (this court will be replaced by a new division, the Business and Property Division, from October 2026)
- the Family Division.

Collectively the three divisions of the High Court hear a wide range of civil cases. It is important to understand that in many cases, the High Court and the County Court have concurrent (parallel) jurisdiction to hear civil cases. The Civil Procedure Rules (together with the accompanying Practice Directions) set out in which court civil proceedings should be started. You can access these resources on the Ministry of Justice's website. You should familiarise yourself with the following general principles (and are advised to check the website regularly to keep abreast of any developments or changes in the guidance).

- If the value of the case is £100,000 or less, it *must* be started in the County Court. This rule applies *unless* the claim involves a claim for damages in respect of personal injuries; in such cases, all claims with a value of £50,000 or less *must* be commenced in the County Court.
- If the value of a claim is more than £100,000 (or £50,000 in cases involving a claim for damages in respect of personal injuries), it *may* be started in the High Court.
- A claimant *may* opt to commence proceedings in the High Court where the claim is complex (for example, the claim has particularly complex facts or involves complex legal issues) or the outcome is important to the public in general. All other cases should be commenced in the County Court rather than the High Court.

It is also worthwhile noting that even if a claim is issued in the High Court, a judge may transfer the case to the County Court if they consider it appropriate to do so.

Revision tip

Remember that in many civil cases, the High Court and County Court have concurrent jurisdiction. Although this technically means that the claimant can choose in which court to commence proceedings, *only* complex cases or those which involve a public interest element and claims with a value or more than £100,000 (or £50,000 in personal injury cases) should start in the High Court. When analysing client-based scenarios in the SQE FLK1 assessment, remember to look out for the following: the value of the claim, whether the claim involves a public interest element and whether there is anything to suggest that the case might be deemed complex. You must also remember that the value limit is lower (£50,000 rather than £100,000) where the claim relates to damages in respect of personal injuries. See ***Revise SQE: Dispute Resolution.***

Procedural link: commencing civil claims

There is a body of rules that govern the administration and management of civil cases. These are known as the Civil Procedure Rules 1998. In the SQE, your knowledge and understanding of these rules is assessed in the civil procedure and dispute resolution sections of the examinations.

King's Bench Division

The King's Bench Division has the most varied jurisdiction of the three divisions. Generally, the King's Bench Division hears contract and tort disputes that are complex and/or involve substantial sums of money.

When the court sits as a Divisional Court of the King's Bench Division, it can hear criminal appeals from the magistrates' court and the Crown Court, and judicial review hearings.

Chancery Division/Business and Property Division

As noted above, the Chancery Division will soon be replaced by the Business and Property Division. This division currently hears business or property disputes that are complex and/or involve substantial sums of money.

Collectively, the term 'Business and Property Courts' refers to a collection of specialist courts which deal with high-value and/or complex commercial, business, property, technology, construction and intellectual property cases. All the Business and Property Courts will be incorporated into the new Business and Property Division when it is established in October 2026.

Family Division

The Family Division has jurisdiction to hear complex family law cases. It has exclusive jurisdiction to hear international child abduction cases and matters that involve the exercise of the High Court's inherent jurisdiction. It is important to note that the Family Division of the High Court and the Family Court are distinct courts. The Family Court is a separate court that hears most family law cases. Some cases that begin in the Family Court but are considered to be very complex can be transferred to the Family Division of the High Court. The Family Division can also hear some appeals from the Family Court.

Family Court

The Family Court, formed in 2014, is the court of first instance for most family law cases. Family law cases typically involve the following matters:

- applications for divorce, dissolution or nullity
- cases concerning financial or childcare arrangements following relationship breakdown
- applications for adoption
- care proceedings.

Cases are allocated by gatekeepers, following the principles laid out in the Family Court Rules 2014. This process ensures that cases are considered by an appropriately experienced judge.

Revision tip

When revising this topic, remember that family law matters will usually be considered by the Family Court in the first instance. Unless the Family Division of the High Court have special jurisdiction in respect of the case (eg it involves international family law or the inherent jurisdiction) it is likely the case will be considered by the Family Court.

County Court

The County Court hears a wide range of civil cases. It is a court of first instance but can also hear appeals in some circumstances. As noted above, claimants in civil cases can *choose* to commence proceedings in the County Court. The County Court tends to hear cases that are less complex and of lower monetary value than those considered by the High Court. As outlined above (**pages 10–11**), the general rule of thumb is that civil cases with a value of £100,000 or less should be commenced in the County Court. In cases involving a claim for damages in respect of personal injury, cases with a value of £50,000 or less should be issued in the County Court.

Tribunals

Some civil cases are considered by tribunals. Tribunals are specialist judicial bodies that adjudicate disputes in specialist areas of law. Technically speaking, tribunals fall outside the formal court structure, but they play an important role in the administration of civil justice. The Tribunals, Courts and Enforcement Act 2007 introduced a two-tiered tribunal system. Generally, the First-Tier Tribunal acts as a court of first instance and the Upper Tribunal deals with appeals from the First-Tier Tribunals. There is also a separate employment tribunal system. Tribunals hear a wide range of cases ranging from employment law matters to appeals relating to immigration, asylum, tax, social entitlement and property matters.

Exam warning

You should *always* read the question carefully and make sure you understand what it requires you to do. In the SQE FLK1 assessment, you may be asked to:

- identity the most suitable venue for a case, or
- identify which statement most accurately identifies the court(s) that has jurisdiction to hear a specific type of case.

You may be thinking, what is the difference between these two questions? The former requires you to exercise your judgement. The latter requires you to accurately identify which of the statements most accurately describes the court(s) that have the legal authority to hear that type of case.

If you are asked to identify the most appropriate court to hear a case, ensure you have carefully analysed the facts to determine:

- the legal issue involved (eg contract, personal injury, childcare arrangements dispute, child abduction case, etc)
- the likely value of the claim (if relevant)
- whether there are any factors which suggest the case is complex.

You will then be able to identify the most suitable venue for the case.

Now put your knowledge to the test and attempt **Practice example 1.2**.

Practice example 1.2

Your client, Edwin, was involved in a road traffic accident last year. He suffered injuries to his neck and left arm that prevented him from being able to work for five months. The other driver has rejected liability for the accident. Edwin is a self-employed builder. As a result of his injuries, he lost around £12,500 of income over the five months he could not work. He wants to make a claim to recover his lost earnings and to claim compensation for the injuries he suffered. The estimated value of the compensation for his injuries is £8,000.

In which court do you think Edwin should issue his claim?

Edwin's case concerns a claim for damages in respect of personal injuries. Such cases are issued in either the High Court or the County Court. Generally speaking, the value of the claim determines which of

these courts should hear the case. Where a matter involves damages for personal injuries valued at £50,000 or less, proceedings are typically issued in the County Court rather than the High Court. The value of Edwin's claim is estimated to be around £20,500. There are no factors to suggest that the case would be particularly complex; the court would simply be required to review the evidence and determine the facts and whether, on the balance of probabilities, the other driver is liable for the accident. For these reasons, the claim should be issued in the County Court.

Summary: civil courts

The High Court, the County Court and the Family Court are often collectively referred to as the 'civil courts' because, as you will now know, they deal with most civil cases.**Figure 1.2** summarises which courts hear which types of civil cases

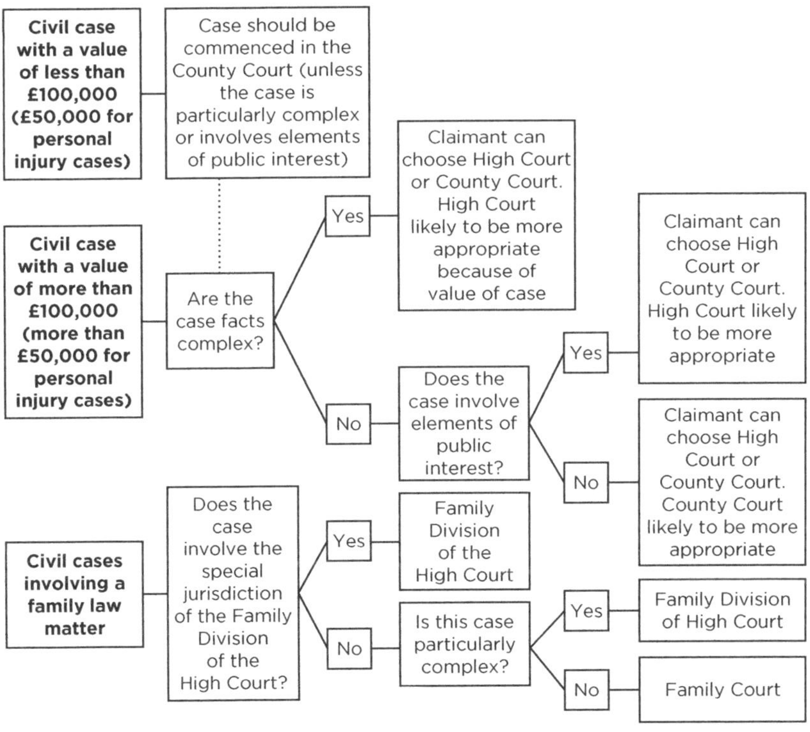

Figure 1.2: Civil courts summary

Crown Court

The Crown Court is typically a court of first instance. It considers criminal law cases. It deals with serious criminal offences and only hears cases where the defendant is accused of committing an indictable offence or a more serious triable either way offence:

- Indictable offences are very serious offences, such as robbery, rape and murder.
- Triable either way offences are offences that can either be considered by the Crown Court or by the magistrates' court, depending on the seriousness of the offence.

A good example of a triable either way offence is theft. In some cases, theft will be considered a serious criminal offence because of the value of the property that was taken and/or because of the circumstances in which it was taken (eg the defendant abused a position of trust). These cases would be considered by the Crown Court. If a defendant appropriated a low-value item from a supermarket, it is likely to be considered by the magistrates' court. The allocation of triable either way offences is discussed below. Because it hears serious criminal cases, trials in the Crown Court have juries.

Magistrates' court

The magistrates' court is a court of first instance. It deals primarily with criminal cases, but it has some *limited* jurisdiction in respect of some civil matters. The magistrates' court also deals with the first appearance of any defendant charged with a criminal offence. It deals with procedural issues and hears initial bail applications.

Criminal jurisdiction of the magistrates' court

- The magistrates' court deals with all cases involving summary offences. Summary offences tend to be less complex and less serious than other types of criminal offences so do not require trial by jury. For example, most motoring offences are summary offences.
- The magistrates' court also has jurisdiction to hear cases involving offences triable either way (eg theft, burglary). In these cases, defendants do *not* have the right to insist on being tried in a magistrates' court, *but the magistrates' court can accept jurisdiction for the case if they feel it is appropriate*.
- For triable either way offences, a defendant can insist on a trial by jury in the Crown Court.

- Where a triable either way case is too serious or too complex to be tried by magistrates, it *must* be sent to the Crown Court for trial.
- The magistrates' court has limited sentencing powers. In particular, the magistrates' court can only order a custodial sentence of up to 6 months (or up to 12 months in total if the defendant has committed multiple triable either way offences).
- When determining whether the magistrates' court has jurisdiction to hear a triable either way offence, the magistrates will consider:
  - the seriousness of the offence
  - any relevant prior convictions
  - whether the sentencing powers they have are likely to be sufficient to deal with the case.
- If the magistrates' court believes its sentencing powers are insufficient to deal with the case, it will reject jurisdiction for the case and the case will be sent to the Crown Court. This is known as the 'allocation' procedure.

Revision tip

In the SQE FLK1 assessment, you might be asked to determine which court would have jurisdiction to hear a criminal case. Remember *all* criminal cases are tried in either the magistrates' court or the Crown Court (save some very rare exceptions that you do not need to familiarise yourself with). **Figure 1.3** illustrates which of the two criminal trial courts have jurisdiction to hear different types of criminal cases. If you are asked to determine which court of first instance is appropriate in a criminal case, you should work through this flow chart.

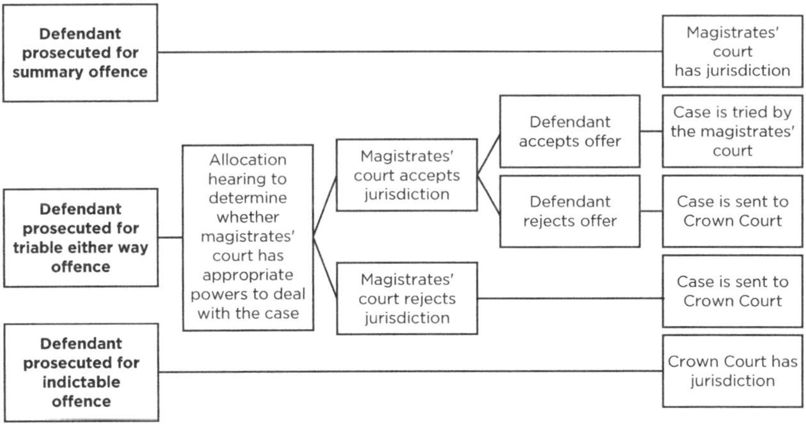

Figure 1.3: Determining the court of first instance in criminal cases

Procedural link: criminal procedure

Criminal procedure is an area of functioning legal knowledge assessed by the SQE. Criminal procedure examines the various procedural rules governing the administration of criminal justice. See ***Revise SQE: Criminal Practice***.

Civil jurisdiction of the magistrates' court

As already noted, the magistrates' court also has a limited civil jurisdiction. Magistrates' courts typically deal with licensing applications and appeals regarding the issuing of pub and restaurant licences.

Youth Court

The Youth Court deals with criminal cases where the defendant is aged between 10 and 17 years old. The Youth Court is designed to be less formal than an adult criminal court and the magistrates who preside over cases receive specialist training. As a general rule of thumb, all criminal cases involving youth defendants should be tried in the Youth Court. Only cases that are very serious and likely to attract a lengthy custodial sentence should be sent to the Crown Court. For example, cases where the defendant has been accused of homicide, manslaughter, rape or firearms offences will be sent to the Crown Court (Crime and Disorder Act 1998, s 51A).

Procedural link: youth justice

There are special procedures that apply during the trial and sentencing of children. These are outside the purview of this book, but you should refer to a criminal procedure book to learn more about the administration of youth justice. See ***Revise SQE: Criminal Practice***.

Now put your knowledge to the test and attempt **Practice example 1.3**.

Practice example 1.3

Elliot has been charged with the offence of theft. He is accused of stealing around £7,000 from a safe at his place of employment. Elliot has several convictions for similar offences. He has entered a plea of 'not guilty' and wants to be tried by a jury in the Crown Court.

Which court would Elliot's case be heard by?

Theft is a triable either way offence. In Elliot's case, the magistrates' court may reject jurisdiction because of the value of the goods stolen and because Elliot's prior convictions are likely to lead to a

higher fine and/or longer sentence that may exceed the sentencing powers available in the magistrates' court. In any event, even if the magistrates' court accepted jurisdiction, the facts suggest that Elliot is likely to decline the offer to have his case tried in the magistrates' court. The case would, therefore, be considered by the Crown Court.

You should now have a good idea of the types of cases that are considered by each court within the court structure. You should now be able to:

- differentiate between civil and criminal cases
- identify which courts hear civil cases in the first instance
- identify which courts hear criminal cases in the first instance
- identify which types of judges sit in each of the courts in the English legal system.

Remember that the parties to a case can, in some circumstances, appeal a court's decision. It is important to understand that there are designated routes of appeal in different types of cases.

THE APPEALS SYSTEM

So far, this chapter has focused on the function and jurisdiction of the various courts that comprise the English legal system. However, it is important to note that in SQE1 you are also required to understand how the appeals system works (eg who may appeal a decision and on what basis, and which court(s) has jurisdiction to consider such an appeal). For the purposes of SQE1, you need to understand how both the civil and criminal appeal systems operate.

To revise these topics, refer to ***Revise SQE: Dispute Resolution*** (civil appeals system) and ***Revise SQE: Criminal Practice*** (criminal appeals system).

Routes of appeal: civil cases

In civil cases, appeals may be made by either party to a dispute. For SQE1, you need to ensure you are aware of the designated routes of appeal available in civil cases. Because this topic is assessed as part of dispute resolution in SQE1, you should refer to ***Revise SQE: Dispute Resolution*** for an overview of the various routes of appeal available in civil cases.

The final topic to discuss in this chapter is **rights of audience**.

Key term: rights of audience

The term 'rights of audience' refers to the right of an advocate to be heard in legal proceedings.

RIGHTS OF AUDIENCE

Finally, it is necessary to understand when legal professionals are able to appear in court to represent their client(s). Advocacy rights refer to the ability of a person to appear in court and present the case of their client. The right to appear in court on behalf of a client is known as having rights of audience. Solicitors are granted rights of audience but must acquire **higher rights of audience** in order to exercise advocacy rights in the 'higher' senior courts. **Table 1.3** summarises the rights of audience for solicitors and barristers. Once you have revised this topic, test your knowledge by answering **Practice example 1.5 (page 22)**.

Table 1.3: Rights of audience

Legal professional	Brief description of role	Rights of audience
Solicitor	Solicitors are typically the first point of contact for individuals seeking legal advice. They undertake a wide range of work. Typically, this involves advising clients, drafting legal documents and undertaking pre-trial case preparation. Nowadays, it often includes appearing in court as a trial advocate. Solicitors are regulated by the Solicitors Regulation Authority (SRA).	Solicitors are granted rights of audience once they are admitted to the roll of solicitors. However, they cannot exercise rights of audience in the higher courts unless they are accredited to do so. Put simply, solicitors may appear on behalf of a client in tribunals and courts such as the magistrates' courts and the County Court (providing they have been admitted to the roll and have a current practising certificate from the SRA). Solicitors *may* also qualify for *higher* rights of audience, which allow them to represent clients in some or all of the following courts: the Crown Court, the High Court, the Court of Appeal, and the Supreme Court. Solicitors may be accredited for higher rights upon successful

Table 1.3: Continued

		completion of an advocacy assessment based on the SRA Higher Rights of Audience competence standards. Note, there are separate awards for rights of audience for criminal and civil advocacy. The SRA Authorisation of Individuals Regulations, which can be accessed on the SRA's website, sets out the education and training requirements for solicitors seeking to exercise higher rights of audience in the higher courts of England and Wales.
Barrister	Barristers are specialist legal advisers and courtroom advocates. They are regulated by the Bar Standards Board (BSB).	Qualified barristers have full rights of audience in all courts. This means they can represent clients and make oral submissions in any court. Note that only qualified barristers have these rights (eg a barrister who has been called to the Bar, holds a current practising certificate from the BSB and is not subject to the 'three year rule', discussed below). It is important to note that the BSB Handbook, which can be accessed via the BSB website, requires newly qualified barristers with less than three years' standing to work with a 'qualified person' when they undertake specified 'reserved legal activities', including the exercise of rights of audience. This is sometimes referred to as the 'three year rule'. The regulation of legal service providers and the meaning of the term 'reserved legal activities' is explored in more detail in **Chapter 5**.

Key term: higher rights of audience

The term 'higher rights of audience' refers to the right to advocate on behalf of the client in senior courts (higher rights of audience were introduced by s 31 of the Courts and Legal Services Act 1990, as amended by the Access to Justice Act 1999).

Exam warning

In order to correctly identify whether a solicitor can exercise rights of audience in a specific case, you will need to ask yourself two questions:

1) Is the case being heard in a senior court?
2) Is the case a civil case or a criminal case?

If the answer to question 1 is yes, a solicitor must have acquired *higher* rights of audience. The answer to question 2 will determine which advocacy assessment the solicitor must have undertaken. For example, if the case is a civil case, the solicitor must have undertaken civil advocacy assessments and been awarded corresponding higher rights of audience in the senior civil courts.

Practice example 1.5

Gerald is a newly qualified barrister (of 18 months standing). He has successfully completed pupillage and has a valid practising certificate. He wants to represent a client in a hearing in the Crown Court.

Can Gerald exercise rights of audience in the Crown Court?

Gerald is a newly qualified barrister. Because he has less than three years' standing, he *must* be supervised and supported by a 'qualified person' when undertaking reserved legal activities, including the exercise of rights of audience.

■ KEY POINT CHECKLIST

This chapter has covered the following key knowledge points. You can use these to structure your revision, ensuring you recall the key details for each point, as covered in this chapter.

- The judiciary of England and Wales is comprised of various types of judges. The judicial hierarchy ranks judges by virtue of the judicial post/office they hold. Typically, judges hear cases/sit in courts that correspond with their position within the judicial hierarchy. For example, the most senior members of the judiciary sit in the higher courts in the court structure (the Supreme Court and the Court of Appeal).

- Each court within the court structure serves an important but distinct role in the administration of justice. The High Court, the County Court and the Family Court tend to deal with most civil cases. The Crown Court and the magistrates' court deal with most criminal cases. The Court of Appeal and the Supreme Court only hear appeal cases.

- Solicitors and barristers assist and advise clients on legal matters. Typically, solicitors deal with a wide range of work and this includes advising clients, drafting legal documents and undertaking pre-trial case preparation. Barristers are specialist legal advisors and advocates. The term 'rights of audience' refers to the right to be heard in legal proceedings. Barristers automatically acquire rights of audience in all courts. Solicitors automatically acquire rights of audience in the lower courts, but they must undertake specialist training to acquire higher rights of audience to appear in any of the senior courts. It is important to remember the right to *exercise* any rights of audience is contingent on having a current practising certificate from the relevant regulatory body (eg the SRA or the BSB). Additionally, newly qualified barristers can only exercise rights of audience without a 'qualified person' once they have three years' standing.

■ KEY TERMS AND CONCEPTS

- judiciary (**page 3**)
- judicial hierarchy (**page 3**)
- jurisdiction (**page 5**)
- standard of proof (**page 6**)
- burden of proof (**page 6**)
- court hierarchy (**page 9**)
- rights of audience (**page 20**)
- higher rights of audience (**page 22**).

SQE1-STYLE QUESTIONS

QUESTION 1

A client intends to apply for a court order to resolve a dispute with her former husband concerning post-divorce childcare arrangements for their three children.

Which of the following courts would hear this case at first instance?

A. The High Court.

B. The County Court.

C. The Family Division of the High Court.

D. The Family Court.

E. The magistrates' court.

QUESTION 2

A defendant is charged with a summary-only offence. They have no previous criminal convictions and want to be tried by jury in the Crown Court.

Which of the following best describes the defendant's right to insist on a trial by jury in these circumstances?

A. The defendant has the right to a trial by jury because they are charged with a criminal offence.

B. The defendant must demonstrate that a trial by jury is both necessary and proportionate in the circumstances.

C. The defendant can only insist on a trial by jury if the magistrates' court rejects jurisdiction for the case.

D. The defendant has the right to a trial by jury if they enter a 'not guilty' plea.

E. The defendant has no right to a trial by jury in these circumstances. The case must be tried summarily in the magistrates' court.

QUESTION 3

A claimant is bringing a case against a defendant, seeking damages for personal injury. The claimant alleges that the defendant caused a road traffic accident. The defendant denies this and refuses to accept responsibility for causing the accident.

Which of the following best describes the burden of proof and standard of proof that the court will apply in deciding the issue?

A. The burden of proof lies with the defendant to prove that they were not responsible for the accident. The standard of proof is the balance of probabilities.
B. The burden of proof lies with the claimant to prove the allegation. The standard of proof is the balance of probabilities.
C. The burden of proof lies with the claimant to prove the allegation beyond a reasonable doubt.
D. The burden of proof lies with the claimant to disprove the defendant's account. The standard of proof is beyond a reasonable doubt.
E. The burden of proof lies with both parties. The claimant must prove the allegation and the defendant must disprove the claimant's allegation. The standard of proof is the balance of probabilities.

QUESTION 4

A client intends to bring a personal injury claim, with an estimated value of between £55,000 and £65,000.

Which of the following statements best describes the most suitable court of first instance for this claim?

A. The High Court.
B. The County Court.
C. The County Court or the High Court.
D. The County Court, the High Court or the Court of Appeal.
E. The Court of Appeal (Civil Division).

QUESTION 5

A solicitor wants to appear in court on behalf of her client in a criminal matter. The case is likely to be considered by the Crown Court at first instance.

Which of the following best describes the solicitor's right to exercise their rights of audience in this matter?

A. The solicitor can appear in the Crown Court on behalf of their client as solicitors are automatically granted rights of audience when they are admitted.

B. The solicitor can appear in the Crown Court on behalf of their client if they have undertaken the relevant assessments in both civil and criminal advocacy and have successfully applied for higher rights of audience.
C. The solicitor can appear in the Crown Court on behalf of their client if they have permission from their client.
D. The solicitor can appear in the Crown Court on behalf of their client if they have undertaken the relevant assessments in criminal advocacy and have successfully applied for higher rights of audience.
E. The solicitor can appear in the Crown Court on behalf of their client as solicitors are automatically granted higher rights of audience when they are admitted.

■ ANSWERS TO QUESTIONS

Answers to 'What do you know already?' questions at the start of the chapter

1) The term 'jurisdiction' refers to the power a court or judge has to hear a case.
2) False. The term 'burden of proof' refers to the party who bears responsibility for proving the case. The degree to which a party must prove their case in order to succeed is the 'standard of proof'.
3) B. The magistrates' court deals with all summary offences and some triable either way offences (if the magistrates' court believes its powers are sufficient to deal with the case).
4) The judicial hierarchy ranks the various members of the judiciary by virtue of the powers and responsibilities associated with each judicial office/post.
5) False. Solicitors are automatically granted rights of audience, but they must *acquire* higher rights of audience to exercise those rights in senior courts.

Answers to end-of-chapter SQE-style questions

Question 1:

The correct answer was D. There are two family courts: the Family Court and the Family Division of the High Court. The Family Court is the default court for most family law cases. The Family Division of the High Court hears a limited range of cases (eg cases involving international child abduction) and some appeals from the Family Court. In this scenario, the client's case concerns a relatively straightforward matter: childcare arrangements following divorce. There are no facts to suggest that the case would need to be heard by the Family Division of the High Court. Options A and C are therefore incorrect. Options B and E are incorrect because neither the County Court nor the magistrates' court has jurisdiction to hear family law matters.

Question 2:

The correct answer was E. In this scenario, the defendant is charged with a summary-only offence. Such cases must be tried summarily in the magistrates' court. This principle applies irrespective of the defendant's wishes or circumstances. The fact that the defendant intends to plead not guilty does not change this position (so option D is incorrect). Option A is incorrect because it suggests that any defendant in any criminal proceedings can elect for trial by jury, which is not the case. Option B is incorrect because summary-only cases are always dealt with by the magistrates' court. It cannot reject jurisdiction for summary-only cases, so option C is also incorrect.

Question 3:

The correct answer was B. In civil cases the burden of proof rests with the claimant. The standard of proof in civil cases is the balance of probabilities.

Question 4:

The correct answer was A. The claim relates to personal injury, so the relevant threshold is £50,000 (rather than the £100,000 threshold that applies in other civil cases). The facts also state that the case is complex. For these reasons, the High Court is likely to be the most appropriate venue. Although the County Court and High Court have concurrent jurisdiction in these types of cases, the question specifically asks you to select the statement which best describes the most appropriate court of first instance for the claim. The complexity and value of the claim suggests the most appropriate court of first instance is the High Court (rather than the County Court). Option B is therefore incorrect. Option C is incorrect because it fails to acknowledge the nature (personal injury), value (above £50,000) and complexity of the claim – it implies either venue would be equally suitable. Options D and E are incorrect because they include the Court of Appeal as a possible venue, but the Court of Appeal is not a court of first instance.

Question 5:

The correct answer was D. In these scenarios, remember to ask yourself (1) Is the case being heard in a senior court? (2) Is the case civil or criminal? The Crown Court is a senior court. The case is a criminal case. This means that the solicitor can appear on behalf of their client only if they have undertaken the relevant assessments in *criminal* advocacy and have successfully applied for *higher* rights of audience in criminal courts.

■ KEY CASES, RULES, STATUTES AND INSTRUMENTS

The SQE1 Assessment Specification does not require you to know any case names or statutory materials for this topic. However, you are advised to familiarise yourself with the relevant provisions of the following statutes:

- Constitutional Reform Act 2005
- Senior Courts Act 1981.

2

Sources of law: primary legislation

MAKE SURE YOU KNOW

It is essential that you, an aspiring solicitor, understand the nature and significance of different types of law. This chapter focuses on *primary legislation*. In England and Wales, the term 'primary legislation' refers to laws passed by Parliament (Acts of Parliament). A significant proportion of the law in England and Wales is contained within Acts of Parliament. All Acts are arranged in a consistent style/format. This chapter explains how primary legislation is created (the 'legislative process') and how statutes are organised/arranged.

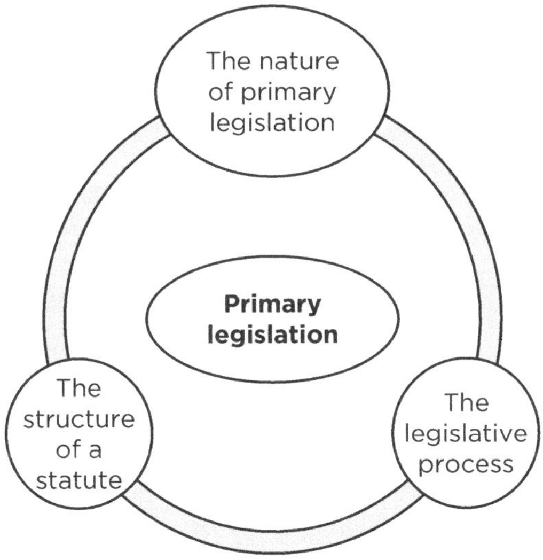

■ SQE ASSESSMENT ADVICE

For the SQE assessments, you are required to understand the legislative process and the structure of an Act of Parliament. In simple terms, you need to know how primary legislation is created and how to read an Act of Parliament.

As you work through this chapter, remember to pay particular attention in your revision to:

- the nature and significance of primary legislation
- the legislative process (how primary legislation is created)
- the structure of an Act of Parliament (how Acts are arranged).

■ WHAT DO YOU KNOW ALREADY?

Have a go at these questions before reading this chapter. If you find some difficult or cannot remember the answers, make a note to look more closely at that during your revision.

1) True or false: an Act of Parliament comes into force on the date it received royal assent.

   [Structure of an Act of Parliament, page 39]

2) What does the second reading stage of the legislative process typically involve?

   [The legislative process, page 34]

3) Which of the following statements is most accurate?

   a) In some limited circumstances, a Bill can become an Act of Parliament without the approval of both Houses of Parliament and/or the monarch.

   b) A Bill cannot become an Act of Parliament unless it has been considered and approved by both Houses of Parliament and the monarch.

   c) In rare and limited circumstances, a Bill can receive royal assent without the approval of the House of Lords.

   [The legislative process, page 34]

4) What is the difference between primary and secondary legislation?

   [What is primary legislation? page 31]

5) True or false: an individual backbench MP can introduce a Bill into the House of Commons.

   [The legislative process, page 34]

WHAT IS PRIMARY LEGISLATION?

An important function of Parliament is to make new laws. The term **legislation** refers to laws passed by Parliament.

Key term: legislation

The term legislation refers to law passed by Parliament (including laws that are passed by virtue of delegated powers on behalf of Parliament).

It is important to note that there are different types of legislation. A significant proportion of the law is contained within **primary legislation**.

Key term: primary legislation

Primary legislation is law passed by Parliament in the form of Acts of Parliament. Acts of Parliament are also commonly referred to as **statutes**.

Key term: statute

The term 'statute' refers to an Act of Parliament. The term 'statutes' is used to refer to more than one Act of Parliament. The term 'statutory' is typically used to refer to something contained within a statute. For example, the phrase 'statutory rights' refers to rights that are contained within an Act/Acts of Parliament. The phrase 'statutory definition' refers to a definition contained within an Act of Parliament.

Primary legislation is the *most* authoritative type of law in England and Wales. This means that where there is a conflict between a statute and any other domestic law, the statute will prevail. **Practice example 2.1** illustrates how this principle might apply in practice.

Practice example 2.1

A judge considering a [fictitious] contract law case must decide whether a term within a contract is 'unfair'. There is a [fictitious] long-standing common law principle which states that unfair terms are not enforceable and numerous cases have defined the meaning of 'unfair' in that context. However, a [fictitious] statute has recently reformed this area of law. The Act states that 'a contractual term will not be legally binding if it is considered unfair'. It also states that 'a term will only be considered unfair if it falls within the definition of "unfair" within this Act'. The Act goes on to define the meaning of the term 'unfair'. The statutory definition of 'unfair' differs from the long-standing common law definition.

Can the judge apply the common law definition rather than the statutory definition?

The statute (the Act of Parliament) clearly states that a contractual term will *only* be considered to be unfair *if* it falls within the definition *within the Act*. This means that the judge *must* apply the statutory definition of the term 'unfair'. The statute is more authoritative than the common law and so the statute prevails.

It is worth highlighting that while statutes are the most authoritative source of law, the judiciary are often required to *interpret and apply* legislation to cases. There are rules governing how judges may interpret and apply the law. This practice is known as statutory interpretation and is discussed in Chapter 3.

Legislation made by the Welsh Parliament

The Welsh Parliament, commonly known as Senedd Cymru or the Senedd, is the democratically elected body that represents the interests of Wales. Part of the Senedd's role is to make laws for Wales. The Senedd is able to pass Acts on any matters that are *not* reserved to the UK Parliament by the Government of Wales Act 2006 (as amended by the Wales Act 2017). Such Acts are referred to as Acts of Senedd Cymru.

Revision tip

The SQE1 Assessment Specification states that you may be assessed on your understanding of the status of the devolved institutions and their relationship with Westminster, and the powers and procedures for the enactment, implementation and repeal of primary and secondary legislation by Westminster and by Senedd Cymru and Welsh Ministers. It is therefore important that you have a good knowledge and understanding of the role, function and law-making powers of the Welsh Parliament. These topics form part of the assessment specification for Constitutional and Administrative Law and EU law and are discussed in detail in ***Revise SQE: Constitutional and Administrative Law***, Chapter 3.

Secondary legislation is law created by government ministers (or other bodies) by virtue of powers given to them by an Act of Parliament (referred to as the 'parent Act'). It is also known as 'delegated' or 'subordinate' legislation. In Wales, ministers in the Senedd make secondary legislation using powers given to them in enabling acts. In both England and Wales, statutory instruments (SIs) are the most common form of secondary legislation.

Key term: secondary legislation

The term 'secondary legislation' refers to laws that are created by government ministers or other bodies by virtue of powers given to them by an Act of Parliament.

Figure 2.1 is a useful illustration that will help you to revise the types of legislation. The next section of this chapter explains how primary legislation is created.

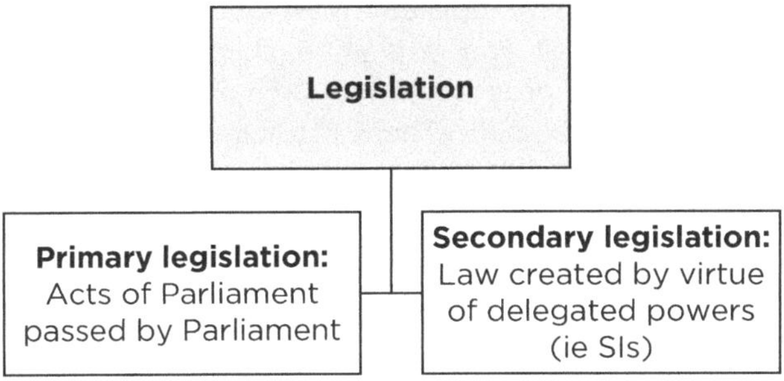

Figure 2.1: Types of legislation

Territorial application of legislation to England and Wales

When determining the extent of an Act of Parliament, it is important to remember that the UK has three separate legal systems: England and Wales, Scotland, and Northern Ireland. If an Act of Parliament *extends* to a jurisdiction, it forms part of the law there. An Act of Parliament may *extend* to the whole of the UK or to one or more of the three jurisdictions within the UK. An Act will usually state which part(s) of the UK it extends to. If an Act of Parliament does not say anything about its extent, it usually extends to the whole of the UK. Acts of Senedd Cymru can *only* extend to England and Wales.

In order for an Act of Parliament to have practical effect in England or Wales, it must extend *and* 'apply' there. The key point is that an Act of Parliament (or specific parts within such an Act) that extends to England and Wales may apply: 1) in relation to *both* England and Wales, 2) *only* in relation to England, or 3) *only* in relation to Wales. Put simply, England and Wales are treated as distinct jurisdictions when determining the application of primary legislation. Primary legislation which is passed by the Senedd can *only* apply to Wales. For this reason, Senedd Acts do not typically include express provisions concerning application.

Revision tip

Make sure that you understand the difference between the terms 'extent' and 'application'. Remember that an Act must extend *and* apply to England/Wales if it is to have practical effect there.

THE LEGISLATIVE PROCESS

The SQE assessments require you to understand the various stages involved in making primary legislation. When revising this topic, make sure that you can recall and explain each stage of the **legislative process**. The legislative process begins with a proposal for a new law being introduced to Parliament. These proposals are known as Bills.

Key term: legislative process

The term 'legislative process' refers to the method used to create primary legislation.

Bills

All statutes begin life as a **Bill**. Bills are typically prepared by the Office of the Parliamentary Counsel (specialists in drafting legislation) and are presented to Parliament for debate. It is important to note that a Bill will *only* become law if it progresses through the legislative process and becomes an Act of Parliament.

Key term: Bill

A Bill is a proposal for a piece of legislation.

It is important to remember that there are different types of Bills. Bills are described as Public Bills, Private Bills or Hybrid Bills. Public Bills are further classified as either government Bills or private members' Bills. **Figure 2.2** provides a useful illustration to help you revise the different types of Bills.

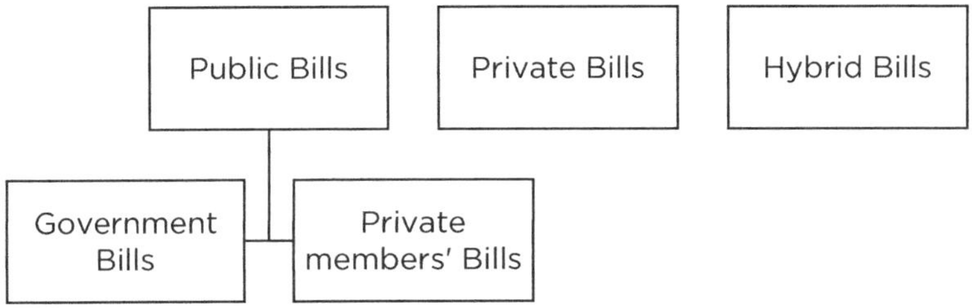

Figure 2.2: Types of Bills

Table 2.1 provides an overview of the various key terms used to describe different types of Bills. Make sure you understand and can recall this information in the SQE FLK1 assessment.

Table 2.1: Key terms: Bills

Key term	Description
• **Public Bill** • **Government Bill** • **Private members' Bill**	**Public Bills** propose new laws, or amend existing laws, that affect the public at large. Public Bills are typically introduced by government ministers and are concerned with implementing the government's legislative programme. These Bills are known as **government Bills**. Most Bills are government Bills. Public Bills that are not introduced by the government are known as **private members' Bills**. As these Bills are not concerned with the implementation of the government's legislative programme, little parliamentary time is allocated to debate them and very few become law.
• **Private Bill**	**Private Bills** are proposed to Parliament by organisations such as local authorities or private companies. These Bills are concerned with gaining parliamentary authority to carry out particular activities or work. As such, they change the law as it applies to a specific individual or organisation, rather than the general public (and are much less common than public Bills).
• **Hybrid Bills**	This type of Bill is rare. An example of such a Bill was the High Speed Rail (West Midlands–Crewe) Bill. It concerned authorisation for the creation of a new railway. The Bill completed the legislative process and is now an Act of Parliament: the High Speed Rail (West Midlands–Crewe) Act 2021.

Revision tip

Do not confuse private members' Bills and private Bills. Private members' Bills are a type of public Bill that propose changes to the law that affects the public at large. Private Bills only impact specific individuals or organisations.

Exam warning

Remember that the SQE1 assessments test your *practical* knowledge and understanding of the FLK topics. You may, therefore, be required to correctly determine what type of Bill is described in a problem-based scenario. When dealing with such a question, remember to ask yourself:

- *Who* introduced the Bill? (Was it the government or an individual MP or Lord?)
- *What* does the Bill propose? (Would it change the law as it applies to the public at large?)

By way of example, if the scenario states that the Bill was introduced by a member of the House of Lords, it would be a private members' Bill. If it is stated that the Bill would change the law as it applies to a specific organisation, it is a private Bill.

Put this tip to the test by trying **Practice example 2.2**.

Practice example 2.2

A backbench MP has proposed a [fictitious] Bill, the 'Criminal Responsibility Bill', to increase the age of criminal responsibility in England and Wales.

What type of Bill is the Criminal Responsibility Bill?

The Bill was proposed by an individual MP rather than the government. It proposes a change to criminal law. It is a private members' Bill.

The process of making primary legislation

Once a proposal to create a new statute has been drafted into a Bill and has been introduced in Parliament, it must pass through several stages of scrutiny before it becomes an Act of Parliament. This process is known as the legislative process. Public Bills may be introduced in either the House of Commons or the House of Lords, but the majority of Bills are introduced in the House of Commons. **Table 2.2** provides

Table 2.2: The legislative process

Stage	Brief overview
First reading	This stage is simply a formality and acts as notification of the proposed law. The short title of the Bill is read out and the date of the second reading is set.
Second reading	At this stage, the policy objectives of the Bill are explained and the objectives and principles of the Bill are debated. After the debate, members vote on whether the Bill should proceed to the next stage.
Committee stage	The Bill is then referred to a committee for detailed examination (in the House of Lords, this stage typically involves the whole House). The committee examines each clause of the Bill and considers whether the clauses are appropriately drafted and whether they are practicable. Amendments to the Bill may be made at this stage. Once a draft Bill is agreed by the committee, it is sent back to the House in the form of a report.
Report stage	The Bill is reprinted, and any amendments are debated and voted upon.
Third reading	At this stage, the Bill is presented to the House for the final time. There may be some debate, but no amendments are made at this stage. Members vote on whether to accept or reject the Bill.
Bill considered by second House	If the Bill proceeds, it is sent to the second House for consideration and approval. If the Bill was introduced in the House of Commons, it will be sent to the House of Lords (and vice versa). The Bill will then progress through the first reading, second reading, committee stage, report stage and third reading in the second House.
Consideration of amendments (ping-pong stage)	This is often referred to as the 'ping-pong' stage. Once the Bill has been through all stages in both Houses, any amendments proposed by the second House need to be considered by the first House. A Bill may go back and forth between each House until both Houses reach agreement on the exact wording of the Bill (hence being referred to as the 'ping-pong' stage). Typically, agreement between the Houses is achieved and the Bill proceeds to royal assent. If agreement is not reached, the Bill may fail to progress further, or, in some limited circumstances, may proceed without the agreement of the House of Lords (see **The Parliament Acts**).
Royal assent	Technically speaking, all legislation requires royal assent to become law. This is when the monarch formally agrees to the Bill becoming an Act of Parliament.

an overview of the stages of the legislative process. It is important to note that a Bill must proceed through *each* stage of legislative process in *both* Houses of Parliament, regardless of which House the Bill is first introduced to. The stages are virtually identical irrespective of whether the Bill is progressing through the House of Commons or the House of Lords. Once the Bill has completed all the parliamentary stages, the monarch must give royal assent (this stage is a formality). Once a Bill receives royal assent, it becomes an Act of Parliament.

In the majority of cases, both Houses of Parliament agree on the final version of the Bill and it receives royal assent and becomes law. There are, however, *rare* circumstances where the Houses reach an impasse. The Parliament Acts, although rarely used, provide a way of resolving such situations. The SQE1 Assessment Specification does not state that you need to cite either of the Parliament Acts. However, you are likely to be assessed on your understanding of the principles contained within those Acts and you may be required to show that you understand how those principles apply to problem-based scenarios.

The Parliament Acts

Historically, the House of Lords had the power to veto Bills. This remained the case until the Parliament Act 1911 was implemented. The Act removed the Lords' power to veto a Bill, unless the Bill was to extend the lifetime of a Parliament. Under the 1911 Act, the Lords could delay a Bill by up to two years. The Parliament Act 1949 reduced the Lords' delaying powers to one year. The Parliament Acts prevent the Lords, the *unelected* chamber of Parliament, from blocking legislation that has the support of the *elected* chamber of Parliament, the House of Commons. As such, the Parliament Acts define the powers of the Lords in relation to public Bills that are introduced in the House of Commons. The key points to remember are as follows:

- Public Bills that begin in the House of Commons can be delayed by the Lords for a maximum of one year. After that, the Bill can be reintroduced and can receive royal assent without the agreement of the House of Lords.
- The Lords do not have the power to delay money Bills for one year. Bills that are concerned with taxes or spending public money must receive royal assent no later than a month after being introduced in the Lords.
- The Parliament Acts cannot be used to enact major constitutional reforms or extend the lifetime of Parliament beyond five years.
- The Parliament Acts do not apply to private Bills or Bills that were introduced in the Lords.

Once the legislative process is complete, the Bill receives royal assent and it becomes an Act of Parliament.

Revision tip

When revising this subject, consider how your knowledge of the legislative process might be assessed in the SQE. For example, you may be required to read some factual information and identify the further steps required for a Bill to become law. It is, therefore, a good idea to practise the *skill* of *applying* your knowledge to problem-based scenarios - you can begin with **Practice example 2.3**.

Practice example 2.3

The government has introduced a [fictitious] Bill to make significant changes to employment law. The Bill is supported by the House of Commons but is opposed in the House of Lords. The Parliament Acts 1911 and 1949 are invoked in order to pass the Bill into law.

What further steps are required for the Bill to become law?

The Parliament Acts limit the powers of the Lords. In the example above, the Bill is a public Bill that began in the House of Commons. Such Bills can be delayed by the Lords for a maximum of one year. After that, the Bill can be reintroduced and can receive royal assent without the agreement of the Lords. This means that the further steps required for the Bill to become law are approval in the House of Commons and royal assent.

STRUCTURE OF AN ACT OF PARLIAMENT

Acts of Parliament are typically organised and presented in a uniform style. You need to familiarise yourself with this structure so that you can find important information within a statute. **Table 2.3** identifies and explains the key features of an Act of Parliament.

Table 2.3: The structure of an Act of Parliament

Feature	Brief overview
The Royal Coat of Arms	The Royal Coat of Arms is attached to all statutes to act as a seal for the legislation. This indicates that the Act has received royal assent from the monarchy.

Table 2.3: Continued

Feature	Brief overview
Short title	All Acts have two titles – the 'short title' and the 'long title'. The short title is a short and more convenient way to refer to an Act. Most statutes will be referred to by their short title (eg Theft Act 1968). The short title is usually stated on the first page of the statute below the Royal Coat of Arms. Each Act also contains a statutory provision confirming what the short title is. This clause will typically begin by stating, 'This Act may be cited as ... .'
Year and chapter number	Modern statutes are cited in accordance with the Parliament Numbering and Citation Act 1962. Put simply, the system requires that statutes are given a sequential number (known as a chapter number) within the year they were enacted. For example, the chapter number of the Theft Act 1968 is 60. This means the Theft Act was the 60th statute to be passed in 1968. The year and chapter number typically appear under the short title on the first page of the statute. The chapter number is often represented as a 'C'.
Long title	The long title is a description of the Act and is stated on the first page of the statute. It is easy to spot because it outlines the purpose of the Act. For example, the long title of the Theft Act 1968 states: 'An Act to revise the law of England and Wales as to theft and similar or associated offences, and in connection therewith to make provision as to criminal proceedings by one party to a marriage against the other, and to make certain amendments extending beyond England and Wales in the Post Office Act 1953 and other enactments; and for other purposes connected therewith'.
Date of royal assent	Each Act states the exact date that it received royal assent. This is typically stated after the long title and is shown in brackets.
Enacting formula	The enacting formula is a short paragraph that precedes the main body of the statute. The enacting formula used in most statutes is: 'BE IT ENACTED by the King's most Excellent Majesty, by and with the advice and consent of the Lords Spiritual and Temporal, and Commons, in this present Parliament assembled, and by the authority of the same, as follows'.

Table 2.3: Continued

Feature	Brief overview
Main body	The main body of an Act of Parliament states the substantive law. The main body of the Act is typically divided into sections, subsections, paragraphs and subparagraphs. Sections are shown in numbers (eg Section 1). Subsections are shown as numbers in brackets (eg s 1(1)). Paragraphs are shown as letters in brackets (eg s 1(1)(a)) and subparagraphs are shown as numerals (eg s 1(1)(a)(iii)). Lengthy and/or complex statutes are sometimes split into parts or chapters too.
Commencement	The commencement date details when the Act will come into force. Often, the Act will state a *specific* commencement date when the Act will come into force. If there is no express commencement date, the Act will be deemed to come into force on the day that it received royal assent. Some Acts will not come into effect until the Act, or a particular section of the Act, has been enacted by a SI. These Acts come into force from 'a date to be appointed'.
Schedules	A statute may have one or more schedules following the main body. These schedules often contain provisions that define or explain terms contained in the main body of the Act.
Explanatory notes	Most Acts are accompanied by explanatory notes. Explanatory notes explain the purpose and effect of the Act in plain, non-technical language.

THE STRUCTURE OF AN ACT OF SENEDD CYMRU

Acts which are passed by Senedd Cymru are generally structured in the same way as Acts of Parliament (as outlined in **Table 2.3** above). They typically include a short title, a long title, the enacting formula (see below), a main body (which is divided and presented in the same way as an Act of Parliament) and a section that outlines commencement details. Senedd Acts often also include schedules and explanatory notes. The enacting formula used for Senedd Acts is as follows: 'Having been passed by Senedd Cymru and having received the assent of His Majesty, it is enacted as follows:'.

Revision tip

When revising this topic, you may find it useful to access or download some real statutes and test your ability to find each of the features listed in **Table 2.3**.

Why not access/download the Human Rights Act 1998 and see if you can find the following features:

- the Royal Coat of Arms
- the short title
- the year and chapter number
- the long title
- the enacting formula.

Now try and answer these questions:

1) What mythical creature is depicted in the Royal Coat of Arms?
2) Which of the following is the correct chapter number: 98, 42 or 1?
3) How many subsections are there in section 1?
4) Which section of the Act deals with declaration of incompatibility?
5) What does Schedule 1 deal with?
6) What is the short title and where in the Act is this stated?
7) When did the Act receive royal assent?

The correct answers are:

1) A unicorn
2) 42
3) Six
4) Section 4
5) The Convention Rights
6) Section 22(1) states that the short title is the Human Rights Act 1998. It is also stated underneath the Royal Coat of Arms
7) 9th November 1998, as shown in brackets after the long title

You should now have a good knowledge and understanding of the nature and significance of primary legislation, the legislative process and the structure of Acts of Parliament. Use the following checklist to remind yourself of the key information covered in this chapter and then test your knowledge by trying the practice SQE-style questions.

KEY POINT CHECKLIST

This chapter has covered the following key knowledge points. You can use these to structure your revision, ensuring you recall the key details for each point, as covered in this chapter.

- A key function of Parliament is to create new laws. Legislation is law that is passed by Parliament (or laws that are passed by virtue of delegated powers for Parliament). Legislation is the most authoritative type of law in England and Wales. Where there is a conflict between statute law and common law, the statute *must* prevail.
- Primary legislation is law passed by Parliament in the form of statutes. Secondary legislation is law passed by virtue of delegated powers for Parliament, rather than by Parliament itself (eg SIs).
- Acts of Parliament may extend to the whole of the UK or to any of the three legal jurisdictions of the UK. When determining the extent of an Act of Parliament, remember that England and Wales are classified as a single jurisdiction.
- Acts of Parliament (or provisions within such Acts) which *extend* to England and Wales may *apply* to both England and Wales, or they may apply only in relation to either England or Wales. Acts of Senedd Cymru extend to England and Wales but can *only* apply to Wales.
- A Bill is a proposal for a new Act of Parliament. All statutes begin as Bills. The majority of Bills considered by Parliament are public Bills. Public Bills are typically introduced by government ministers in the House of Commons and seek to introduce or amend laws that impact the public generally.
- The process of creating statutes is known as the legislative process. In summary, this involves the Bill being considered and debated in both the House of Commons and the House of Lords. Once agreement between the Houses has been reached, the Bill receives royal assent and becomes an Act of Parliament.
- Most Bills are introduced in the House of Commons, so are debated and considered there first. The stages of the legislative process are then repeated in the House of Lords. The key stages in the legislative process are: first reading and second reading, committee stage, report stage, third reading, royal assent.
- Because members of the House of Lords are not elected by the public, its powers to veto or delay legislation that has been approved by the House of Commons is limited. Public Bills can be delayed by the Lords for a maximum of one year. 'Money' Bills that are concerned

with taxes or spending public money can only be delayed for up to one month.
- Acts of Parliament are arranged in a uniform format.

KEY TERMS AND CONCEPTS

- legislation (**page 31**)
- primary legislation (**page 31**)
- statute (**page 31**)
- secondary legislation (**page 33**)
- legislative process (**page 34**)
- Bill (**page 34**)
- public Bill (**page 35**)
- government Bill (**page 35**)
- private members' Bill (**page 35**)
- private Bill (**page 35**)
- hybrid Bill (**page 35**)

SQE1-STYLE QUESTIONS

QUESTION 1

The government has introduced a Bill that will change national taxation policy. The Bill has passed through the House of Commons but is opposed in the House of Lords. The Parliament Acts 1911 and 1949 are invoked in order to pass the Bill into law.

Which of the following statements most accurately outlines the requirements that need to be satisfied in order for the Bill to become law?

A. The Bill is a public Bill so both Houses of Parliament will need to reach agreement on the Bill before it can receive royal assent.

B. The House of Lords can delay the Bill for a maximum of one month. After that, the Bill can receive royal assent without the approval of the House of Lords.

C. The House of Lords can delay the Bill for a maximum of two years. After that, the Bill can receive royal assent without the approval of the House of Lords.

D. The Bill is a private Bill and both Houses of Parliament will need to reach agreement on the Bill before it can receive royal assent.

E. The House of Lords can delay the Bill for a maximum of one year. After that, the Bill can receive royal assent without the approval of the House of Lords.

QUESTION 2

A [fictitious] Act of Parliament has recently been enacted. The Act is known as the 'Education Act 2025'. Under the words 'Education Act 2025', the following information is stated:

2025 c.45
[12 November 2025]

Which of the following statements most accurately describes 'The Education Act 2025'?

A. The long title of the Act is the 'Education Act 2025 The Act is deemed to be in force from 12 November 2025. The Act was passed on the 45th day in 2025.
B. The short title of the Act is the 'Education Act 2025'. The Act received royal assent on 12 November 2025. The Act was passed on the 45th day in 2025.
C. The short title of the Act is the 'Education Act 2025'. The Act is deemed to be in force from 12 November 2025. The Act was passed on the 45th day in 2025.
D. The short title of the Act is the 'Education Act 2025'. The Act received royal assent on 12 November 2025. The Act was the 45th Act passed by Parliament in 2025.
E. The long title of the Act is the 'Education Act 2025'. The Act received royal assent on 12 November 2025. The Act was the 45th Act passed by Parliament in 2025.

QUESTION 3

A highly [fictitious] controversial Act changed the legal test for 'dishonesty' in theft cases. The statutory test for dishonesty has attracted significant criticism and there is a growing pressure on the government to reform the law in this area.

Which of the following statements most accurately describes the legal effect of the Act?

A. The Act is in force and the statutory test for dishonesty must be applied by judges hearing criminal law cases unless and until the law is changed by Parliament.

B. The Act is in force but the statutory test for dishonesty may be overturned if the matter is considered by the Court of Appeal or the Supreme Court.
C. The Act is in force and the statutory test for dishonesty must be applied by judges hearing theft cases unless and until the law is changed by Parliament.
D. The Act is in force and the statutory test for dishonesty may be applied by judges hearing theft cases unless and until the law is changed by Parliament.
E. The Act is in force but the statutory test for dishonesty may be overturned if the matter is considered by the Supreme Court.

QUESTION 4

A Bill that proposes to extend the lifetime of Parliament to six years has been proposed by the government. The Bill has completed its passage through the House of Commons but is opposed by the House of Lords.

Which of the following statements most accurately describes the steps that may be taken to pass the Bill into law?

A. The House of Commons has the power to bypass the requirement for approval of the House of Lords.
B. The House of Commons does not have the power to bypass the requirement for approval of the House of Lords.
C. The House of Commons has the power to bypass the requirement for approval of the House of Lords if the Bill has been delayed by more than one year.
D. The House of Commons has the power to bypass the requirement for approval of the House of Lords if the Bill has the overwhelming support of the House of Commons.
E. The House of Commons has the power to bypass the requirement for approval of the House of Lords if the Bill has been delayed by more than one month.

QUESTION 5

A client has approached a solicitor for advice. The solicitor has identified a statute that is likely to be relevant to the client's case. The solicitor needs to check whether the Act has come into effect.

Which of the following statements most accurately describes the part of the Act that describes when and how the Act will come into force?

A. The explanatory notes will explain the purpose and scope of the Act and will state when the Act comes into effect.

B. The relevant government minister is responsible for determining when the Act comes into effect.

C. The Act will come into effect on the date that is specified in the commencement section of the Act. If there is no commencement section, the Act will be deemed in force from the date it completed the parliamentary stages of the legislative process.

D. The date of royal assent is stated at the beginning of the Act. The date the Act received royal assent will usually be the date that the Act comes into effect.

E. A commencement section within the Act will typically outline how and when the Act comes into effect. The Act may come into effect as a whole or in stages, and may come into effect immediately, on a specified date or on a date to be determined by the relevant government department.

ANSWERS TO QUESTIONS

Answers to 'What do you know already?' questions at the start of the chapter

1) False: some Acts of Parliament do come into effect from the date of royal assent, but this is not the case for many statutes. Many statutes come into force on a specified date or will not come into effect until the Act (or part of the Act) has been enacted by a SI.
2) The second reading stage is an important stage in the legislative process. At this stage the policy objectives and principles of the Bill are debated. After the debate, members vote on whether the Bill should proceed to the next stage.
3) The answer is (c). Usually both Houses of Parliament and the monarch must approval a Bill before it can become an Act of Parliament. If the Parliament Acts are invoked, some Bills can proceed to royal assent without the approval of the House of Lords. In practice, this is rare.

4) Primary legislation is law passed by Parliament in the form of statutes. Secondary legislation is law created by ministers or other bodies under powers given to them by an Act of Parliament.
5) True. An individual backbench MP can introduce a Bill into the House of Commons. Such Bills are referred to as private members' Bills.

Answers to end-of-chapter SQE1-style questions

Question 1:

The correct answer was B. The House of Lords can delay the Bill for a maximum of one month. After that, the Bill can receive royal assent without the approval of the House of Lords. This is because the Bill would be classified as a 'money' Bill. The Parliament Acts prevent the Lords from delaying money Bills for longer than one month.

Question 2:

The correct answer was D. The 'Education Act 2025' is the short title, rather than the long title (therefore options A and E are wrong). The '2025 c.45' indicates the year the Act was passed and the chapter number. The chapter number indicates that it was the 45th Act to be passed in 2025 (as opposed to the 45th day, therefore options B and C are incorrect). The date shown in brackets is the date on which the Act received royal assent.

Question 3:

The correct answer was C. The Act is in force and the statutory test for dishonesty must be applied by judges hearing theft cases unless and until the law is changed by Parliament. The role of the judiciary is to interpret and apply the law laid out in statutes, not to override it (therefore options B and E are wrong). The law remains in force unless and until Parliament changes it. Option A is incorrect because it states the test must be applied in all criminal law cases, which is inaccurate (the Act lays out the test for dishonesty in *theft* cases). Option D is incorrect because it states that judges 'may' apply the test.

Question 4:

The correct answer was B. The House of Commons does not have the power to bypass the requirement for approval of the House of Lords. This is because the Bill seeks to extend the lifetime of Parliament beyond five years. The powers that the House of Commons have to bypass the requirement for approval of the House of Lords cannot be used to enact proposals to extend the lifetime of Parliament beyond five years.

Question 5:

The correct answer was E. The commencement section outlines when and how an Act is to come into force. Option A is incorrect as the explanatory notes have no legal effect and merely provide a description or explanation behind an Act's intention. Option B is incorrect, as while the relevant government minister is responsible in some way, the question asks which part of the Act describes when and how the Act will come into force. Option D is wrong in that royal assent will not usually be the date that the Act comes into force. Option C is wrong because it does not accurately explain the operation of the commencement section.

■ KEY CASES, RULES, STATUTES AND INSTRUMENTS

The SQE1 Assessment Specification does not require you to know any case names, or statutory materials, for this topic. You are, however, expected to be familiar with the legal principles and rules outlined in the chapter.

3

Sources of law: statutory interpretation

MAKE SURE YOU KNOW

A large proportion of law is contained in primary legislation. This type of law is the most authoritative source of law in the UK. This is because the principle of parliamentary sovereignty dictates that Parliament is the highest legal authority in the UK. The primary role of the judiciary is to *apply* the law. Sometimes, this task is much more complex than you might imagine. This is because in many cases the precise scope or effect of a statute is unclear or uncertain. In such cases, judges must try to work out what Parliament intended when it created the law in question, and they do this by interpreting the relevant statute. This process is known as statutory interpretation. This chapter will outline the rules of statutory interpretation and the various tools and aids that judges may use to assist them with statutory interpretation.

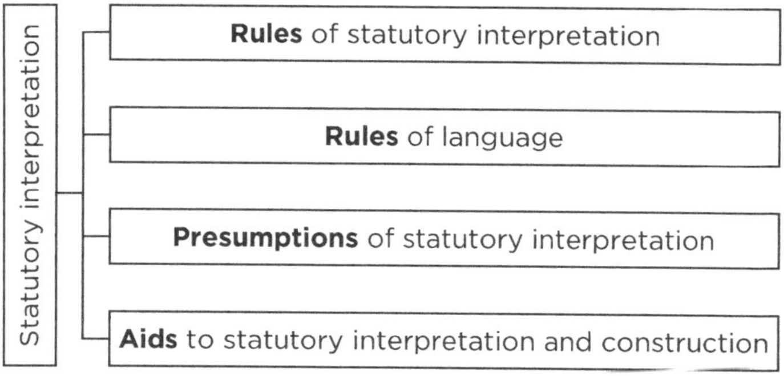

SQE ASSESSMENT ADVICE

For the SQE, you will need to be familiar with the concept of statutory interpretation. Put simply, you need to know how judges approach statutory interpretation and what 'tools' they have at their disposal to assist them with statutory interpretation. When revising this topic, you may find it more manageable to learn the subject in four subtopics, as shown in the diagram above. This topic could be assessed in a number of ways. For example, you may be asked to identify which of the four rules of statutory interpretation has been applied by a judge, or you may also be asked to determine whether a specific aid could be used by a judge to assist with statutory interpretation.

As you work through this chapter, remember to pay particular attention in your revision to:

- the golden rule
- the mischief rule
- the literal rule
- the purposive approach
- presumptions of statutory interpretation
- internal/intrinsic aids to statutory interpretation and construction
- external/extrinsic aids to statutory interpretation and construction.

■ WHAT DO YOU KNOW ALREADY?

Have a go at these questions before reading this chapter. If you find some difficult or cannot remember the answers, make a note to look more closely at that during your revision.

1) True or false? The courts must apply a purposive approach to statutory interpretation.

   [Rules of statutory interpretation, page 52]

2) Which of the following are internal/intrinsic aids to statutory interpretation?
   a) Explanatory notes
   b) Long title
   c) Hansard
   d) Academic textbooks
   e) Dictionaries
   f) Schedules within a statute.

   [Aids to interpretation, page 58]

3) Which rule of statutory interpretation do the courts typically apply first?
   a) Golden rule
   b) Literal rule
   c) Mischief rule
   d) Purposive approach.

   [Rules of statutory interpretation, page 52]

4) True or false? The rule in *Pepper v Hart* [1993] AC 593 abolished the principle that prohibited courts from consulting Hansard to assist with statutory interpretation and construction.

   [Aids to interpretation, page 58]

5) Which rule of statutory interpretation did the court apply in the case of *Smith v Hughes* [1960] 1 WLR 830?

   [Rules of statutory interpretation, page 52]

STATUTORY INTERPRETATION: OVERVIEW

The majority of statutes are drafted by the Office of the Parliamentary Counsel, specialists in drafting legislation (see **Chapter 2**). Despite the great care and skill exercised when drafting legislation, and the thorough scrutiny that occurs as the Bill makes its way through the parliamentary stages of the legislative process, it is often the case that the exact meaning or effect of a specific word, phrase or section within a statute is unclear. This uncertainty may arise because a word or term used in the statute is vague, broad or ambiguous, or because a word has been omitted because the draftsperson thought it would be implied. The uncertainty may also arise because the meaning of the word(s) used in the statute have changed over time. These are just a few of the reasons why the precise meaning or effect of a statute may be unclear. The primary role of the judiciary is to *apply* the law. If the law is unclear, judges must also *interpret* the law. To put it another way, judges must try to ascertain what Parliament intended when the statute was passed so that they can apply the law accordingly. This process is known as **statutory interpretation**. The judiciary interpret statutes by following 'rules' of interpretation. There are also a number of aids, presumptions and rules of language that assist judges in interpreting the law. This next section of this chapter deals with the four 'rules' of statutory interpretation.

Key term: statutory interpretation

The term 'statutory interpretation' refers to the process that judges undertake to interpret the meaning of a word, phrase or section within a statute.

RULES OF STATUTORY INTERPRETATION

There are four 'rules' of statutory interpretation. These rules are also sometimes referred to as rules of construction. The use of the word 'rule' in this context is far from ideal; the rules are better viewed as approaches to statutory interpretation that have been adopted by the courts. The four rules of statutory interpretation are illustrated in **Figure 3.1** and are discussed in more detail below. When revising this topic, ensure you can recall and explain each of the four rules.

Literal rule → Golden rule → Mischief rule → Purposive approach

Figure 3.1: Rules of statutory interpretation

The literal rule

The courts first apply the **literal rule**. This rule requires courts to interpret statutes in a literal manner. In other words, judges should give the words used in the statute their usual/ordinary meaning. Wherever possible, the courts should apply the literal interpretation of the word(s) in the statute. In many cases, the application of the literal rule ensures that the will of Parliament is fulfilled. However, on occasion, the application of the literal rule has resulted in some rather odd outcomes! For example, *Whiteley v Chappell* (1868) LR 4 QB 14 concerned the interpretation of a statute designed to prevent electoral misconduct. The statute stated that it was an offence to impersonate 'any person entitled to vote'. The defendant impersonated a dead person. The courts applied the literal meaning of the words and the defendant was acquitted because a dead person was not a 'person entitled to vote'.

> **Key term: literal rule**
>
> The literal rule is a rule of statutory interpretation. It requires courts to give the words used in a statute their ordinary meaning.

The golden rule

The **golden rule** requires that words in a statute are given their ordinary and literal meaning *unless* that would produce an *absurd* or *repugnant* outcome. What might constitute an 'absurd' or 'repugnant' outcome? In *Re Sigsworth* [1935] 1 Ch 98, a son murdered his mother. His mother had not made a will, and so under the rules relating to intestacy he was entitled to receive her estate as her only child. The application of the literal rule would have produced a *repugnant* outcome because it would have given the son - the murderer - the right to claim the deceased's estate. The court applied the golden rule and held that the principle of public policy that precluded a murderer from claiming a benefit conferred on him by his victim's will also precluded him from claiming a benefit conferred on him by the Administration of Estates Act 1925. In *Maddox v Storer* [1963] 1 QB 451, the defendant had driven a minibus at a speed exceeding 30 mph. The Road Traffic Act 1960 made it an offence to drive a vehicle 'adapted to carry more than seven passengers' at more than 30 mph. The court applied the golden rule and held that the term 'adapted' meant 'suitable or apt' to carry seven or more passengers. A literal interpretation of the word 'adapted' would have produced an *absurd* result because it would have *excluded* all vehicles that were *designed*, rather than *adapted*, to carry more than seven passengers.

Key term: golden rule

The golden rule is a rule of statutory interpretation. It allows courts to depart from the literal interpretation of a statute in order to avoid an absurd or repugnant outcome.

Exam warning

In the SQE, look out for words such as 'absurd' or 'repugnant'. Such words may be used to suggest that a judge has applied the golden rule to avoid an absurd or repugnant outcome that would have arisen from a literal interpretation of the word(s).

The mischief rule

The **mischief rule** derives from *Heydon's Case* [1584] 76 ER 637. It permits judges to consider the 'mischief' that a statute was designed to remedy and interpret the statute in such a way as to address that mischief. To put it more simply, judges may consider the 'problem' that Parliament was aiming to tackle when it passed the statute and interpret the statute in the light of that aim. This rule tends to be applied where a literal interpretation of the statute would create an unintended and obvious 'gap' in the law, as is demonstrated in *Smith v Hughes* [1960] 1 WLR 830. The Street Offences Act 1959 made it an offence for a prostitute to solicit potential customers in a 'street or public place'. In this case, the prostitute solicited business from her home by tapping on a window to attract the attention of people passing by. Under a literal interpretation of the statute, she could not be said to be soliciting in a 'street or public place' since she was inside her house. The 'mischief' that the Act was aiming to address was street prostitution. The court therefore applied the mischief rule and interpreted the words 'street or public place' as including the defendant's home because she was still able to successfully solicit people who were on the street.

Key term: mischief rule

The mischief rule is a rule of statutory interpretation. It allows courts to interpret the meaning of a provision within a statute in the light of the 'mischief' that the Act aimed to address.

The purposive approach

The final rule of statutory interpretation is the **purposive approach**. This approach is much wider than the mischief rule, as the courts may consider the wider aim(s) of the relevant statute. The case of *Pepper v Hart* [1993] AC 593 illustrates the broad scope of the purposive approach.

Mr Hart was a teacher at a public school. As a benefit of the job, his children could attend the school at a significantly discounted rate. The Finance Act 1976 required employees to pay tax on such benefits. The amount of tax payable was based on the cost to the employer of providing the benefit. Mr Hart argued that the reduced fee paid to the school covered the additional costs of having his children educated there. The Inland Revenue, however, contended that Mr Hart should pay tax on the basis of the amount it saved him on the actual cost of sending his children to the school. When the Finance Act 1976 was debated in Parliament, the then Secretary to the Treasury had specifically stated that where the cost of a benefit to an employer was minimal, employees should not have to pay full tax on the benefit. The key legal issue was whether the courts could consult Hansard to help them interpret the purpose of a statute. The House of Lords ruled that Hansard could be consulted in prescribed circumstances (see **aids to interpretation**). Importantly, the statements confirmed that Parliament's intention was for tax to be calculated on the basis of the *additional* costs incurred by the employer in providing the benefit to the employee, and the court interpreted the statute accordingly.

Key term: purposive approach

The purposive approach is a 'rule' of statutory interpretation. When applying this approach, courts consider the purpose of the Act when interpreting the meaning of a provision within the statute.

Revision tip

Ensure you familiarise yourself with the case of *Pepper v Hart*. It not only provides a useful demonstration of how the purposive approach operates, but it also outlines the limited circumstances in which the court may refer to Hansard to assist with statutory interpretation. You do not need to be able to cite this case, but you will be expected to know the relevant principles.

Practice example 3.1 illustrates how your knowledge of the rules of statutory interpretation may be assessed in the SQE1 assessments.

Practice example 3.1

During the course of a [fictitious] trial, a judge is required to interpret the precise meaning of a provision within a statute. The provision includes the following definition: 'any weapon or implement that has been modified so as to make it capable of being used as a weapon'. The defendant was carrying a toy gun filled with acid. The judge must determine whether a toy gun could be classified as an 'implement' and whether it can be said to have been 'modified'. In construing the provision, the judge considers that the statute was designed to reduce the prevalence of attacks involving dangerous makeshift weapons. The judge interprets the words 'implement modified to be used as a weapon' as including the toy gun filled with acid.

Which rule of statutory interpretation has the judge used to interpret the statute?

Here the judge has applied the mischief rule. The judge has taken account of the 'mischief' that the statute sought to address and has interpreted the provision in a way that is consistent with that aim.

RULES OF LANGUAGE

As well as rules of statutory interpretation, there are also **rules of language**.

Key term: rules of language

Rules of language are rules that judges may apply to assist them in interpreting unclear, ambiguous or vague word(s) in the context of other language used within the same statute.

The key rules of language are outlined in **Table 3.1** (see also **Practice example 3.2**).

Table 3.1: The key rules of language

Rule of language	Meaning	Worked example
Ejusdem generis	'of the same type' If an Act includes specific words that are followed by general words, the general words are taken to refer only to things of the same kind	If an Act required 'dogs, cats, guinea pigs, hamsters and other animals' to be registered with a veterinary practice, the general term 'other animals' would be taken to mean other animals of the same type (eg other domestic animals or pets). It would not be taken to include wild animals.
Expressio unius est exclusio alterius	'to express one thing is to exclude others' If an Act expressly lists certain things this implies other things are excluded	If an Act required owners of 'Dobermans, Rottweilers, bulldogs and bull terriers' to keep their dog on a leash in all public parks, this would only apply to owners of the specific breeds listed. The fact the Act includes a complete list of specific breeds implies that all other breeds of dog are excluded.
Noscitur a sociis	'known by the company it keeps' The words used within a statute derive meaning from the words surrounding them.	If an Act mentioned that certain breeds of dog should be kept on a leash in/on 'public parks, beaches and gardens', it would be reasonable to assume that the word 'gardens' referred to public gardens but not private gardens. The words surrounding the term 'gardens' refer to public places, so the term garden should be interpreted in light of that fact.

Practice example 3.2

A [fictitious] statute states that 'sailboats, yachts and fishing boats' must be insured against loss and damage.

Applying the rules of language to this specific provision, would a barge need to be insured against loss or damage?

The *ejusdem generis* rule does not apply because there is no general term (such as 'and other similar boats') to interpret. The *expressio unius est exclusion alterius* rule would apply. The statute explicitly lists specific types of boats. The specific reference to those boats implies other types of boats are excluded. The *noscitur a sociis* rule does not need to be considered since it is not necessary to interpret any of the words in the statute.

PRESUMPTIONS

Courts also apply various common-law presumptions when interpreting statutes. Courts begin by presuming that certain things are implied in *all* statutes. The main presumptions are outlined in **Figure 3.2**. It is important to remember that these presumptions are *rebuttable*. A presumption may be rebutted if the Act expressly goes against one of the presumptions. For example, an Act might specifically state that certain provisions apply retrospectively.

Key term: presumptions of statutory interpretation/construction

This term refers to the common law presumptions that courts presume are implied in all legislation. The presumptions are rebuttable.

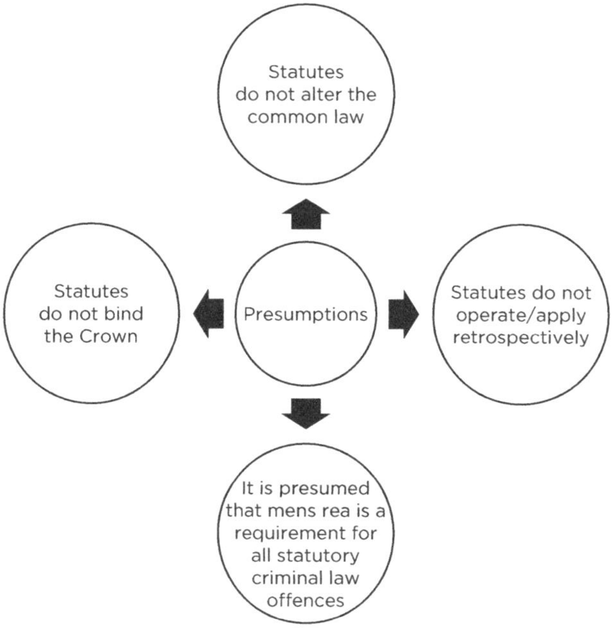

Figure 3.2: Presumptions of statutory interpretation/construction

AIDS TO INTERPRETATION

Finally, courts may also use a range of 'aids' to help them interpret a statute (see **Figure 3.3**). Some of these aids are contained in the statute itself and are known as internal or intrinsic aids to statutory interpretation. All other aids that courts may use are classified as external or extrinsic aids to statutory interpretation.

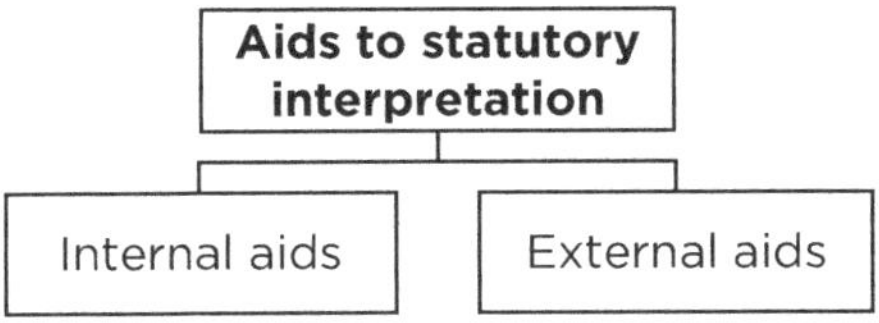

Figure 3.3: Aids to statutory interpretation

Key term: aids to statutory interpretation

Aids to statutory interpretation are things that judges may use to assist them in construing a statute. Aids are classified as either internal or external aids, depending on whether they are located within, or outside of, the statute.

Internal aids

Judges may refer to various internal aids to assist them in interpreting a particular provision of a statute. These are outlined in **Figure 3.4**.

Internal aids to statutory interpretation (intrinsic aids)	Short title	As the short title is very brief, they do not tend to be a useful source of information. However, they do helpfully summarise the overall purpose of the statute.
	Long title	The long title is a description of the Act. It can be a useful tool to ascertain what the statute aimed to achieve.
	Preamble	These do not tend to appear in modern statutes, but they can provide useful context for older statutes.
	Marginal notes	Marginal notes are included for ease of reference but they can help the reader to understand the purpose of a specific provision.
	Punctuation	The punctuation that is used with a provision can help the court to interpret its meaning or scope.
	Schedules	A statute may have one or more schedules following the main body. These schedules often contain provisions that define or explain terms contained in the main body of the Act.
	Examples within the Act	Some Acts include specific examples of how a provision may apply. Such examples can help a judge to interpret a statutory provision.

Figure 3.4: Internal aids

External aids

There are also a number of external aids that judges may use to help interpret a statute. The key external aids are listed and explained in **Table 3.2**.

Table 3.2: Key external aids

External aid	Use of aid
Dictionaries	Judges may consult a dictionary in order to clarify the meaning of a word used within a statute. This can be a useful tool when a judge is trying to ascertain the 'ordinary' meaning of a word.
Interpretation Act 1978	This statute was passed in order to assist judges to interpret common words used in statutes. For example, the Act states that words importing the masculine gender include the feminine (and vice versa) and words in the singular include the plural (and vice versa).
Explanatory notes	Most Acts are accompanied by explanatory notes. Explanatory notes explain the purpose and effect of the Act in plain, non-technical language. They can be a useful tool for ascertaining the intended aim(s) of a statute.
Hansard	Hansard is the official report of what has been debated in the Houses of Parliament. It is updated on a daily basis and is available to access online via Parliament's website. Historically, judges were prohibited from referring to Hansard; however, this rule was *relaxed* by the rule in *Pepper v Hart*. Judges may refer to Hansard *only* where the following are satisfied: • the case involves legislation that is ambiguous or obscure or leads to an absurdity • the material relied on consists of statements made in Parliament by ministers or other promoters of the Bill • the statements relied upon are clear and can assist the court in construing the relevant legislation. It is very important to remember that *all* three of the requirements listed above must be satisfied in order for a judge to rely on Hansard. Judges cannot refer to Hansard in cases where the statute is clear and unambiguous.
Academic writings	A judge may refer to academic writings. For example, a textbook or journal article written by a prominent academic in the field.

Table 3.2: Continued

External aid	Use of aid
Treaties and conventions	Courts may refer to international treaties and conventions when interpreting legislation. It is important to note that s3 of the Human Rights Act (HRA) 998 expressly requires that, as far as it is possible to do so, domestic courts interpret statutes in a way that is compatible with the European Convention on Human Rights (ECHR). If a court cannot interpret legislation in a way that is compatible with the ECHR, they can issue a declaration of incompatibility under s4 of the HRA 1998. In the SQE, your understanding of the HRA 1998 and its impact on domestic law is assessed as part of constitutional and administrative law. Make sure that you familiarise yourself with this topic ahead of the SQE.

Key term: the rule in *Pepper v Hart*

In *Pepper v Hart* [1993] AC 593, the House of Lords held that Hansard could be consulted as an external aid to statutory interpretation where specific criteria are satisfied; this is referred to as the 'rule in *Pepper v Hart*'.

It is important that you familiarise yourself with the various internal and external aids to statutory interpretation. To test your ability to answer a problem-based question on this topic, try **Practice example 3.3**.

Practice example 3.3

A judge is considering a case concerning the interpretation of the legislation governing divorce. The area of law is widely considered to be outdated and the judge is aware that Parliament has recently debated changing the law in this area.

Can the judge refer to such debates in order to assist with interpreting the relevant statute?

The recent debates have no bearing on how the statute ought to be interpreted. The judge cannot consider the recent debates concerning possible law reform when interpreting the statute. If Parliament wishes to change the law, it must do so by virtue of new legislation.

INTERPRETATION OF LEGISLATION MADE BY SENEDD CYMRU

The rules of statutory interpretation outlined in this chapter also apply to the interpretation of legislation made by Senedd Cymru. The Legislation (Wales) Act 2019 aimed to standardise how certain terms, provisions and rules are understood and applied across all Acts of Senedd Cymru and subordinate Welsh legislation. It also provides guidance on the interpretation of Welsh laws. For example, s 7 states that words in the singular include the plural and vice versa, and, importantly, the table set out in Schedule 1 defines a number of key terms and phrases. For example, it defines 'month' as 'a calendar month'.

It is also worthwhile remembering that Senedd Cymru can only make legislation which is within its legislative competence. For this reason, the Government of Wales Act 2006 requires that any legislative provision (including subordinate legislation) which *could* be read in such a way as to be outside the Senedd's legislative competence, *must* be 'read as narrowly as is required for it to be within competence or within the powers, if such a reading is possible, and is to have effect accordingly'.

■ KEY POINT CHECKLIST

This chapter has covered the following key knowledge points. You can use these to structure your revision, ensuring you recall the key details for each point, as covered in this chapter.

- A primary function of Parliament is to make and amend laws. A significant proportion of such laws are contained within primary legislation (statutes). This type of law is the most authoritative type of law in England and Wales.
- The primary function of the judiciary is to apply statute law to cases. Sometimes this task is complicated by the fact that the statute in question is unclear or ambiguous. This may be because a word or words used in the statute is/are vague, broad or ambiguous, or because the meaning of the word(s) used in the statute have changed over time. In such cases, judges must *interpret* the law. This process is known as statutory interpretation.
- The principle of parliamentary sovereignty dictates that Parliament is the supreme law-making body in England and Wales. The judiciary must, therefore, try to interpret statute law in accordance with what Parliament intended when the statute was passed. Over the years, the courts have developed four rules of statutory interpretation to assist

them in this task: the literal rule, the golden rule, the mischief rule and the purposive approach.
- The courts may also apply rules of language to assist with statutory interpretation. These rules of language help courts to interpret the meaning or scope of specific legislative provisions by examining other language used in the statute.
- There are a number of rebuttable presumptions that courts presume are implied in all statutes. These presumptions are presumed to be implied in all statutes unless the relevant statute expressly declares otherwise.
- Finally, the courts may also use aids to help them interpret a statute. These aids are categorised as internal aids and external aids. Internal aids are those found within the statute itself. External aids are not contained within the statute.

■ KEY TERMS AND CONCEPTS

- statutory interpretation (**page 52**)
- literal rule (**page 53**)
- golden rule (**page 54**)
- mischief rule (**page 54**)
- purposive approach (**page 55**)
- rules of language (**page 56**)
- presumptions of statutory interpretation/construction (**page 58**)
- aids to statutory interpretation (**page 59**)
- the rule in *Pepper v Hart* (**page 61**)

■ SQE1-STYLE QUESTIONS

QUESTION 1

During the course of a criminal trial, a judge is required to interpret the precise meaning of a word used within a statute. The judge first looks at the natural ordinary meaning of the word used. However, such an interpretation of the word would lead to a repugnant outcome. The judge therefore interprets the words in a different way, which does not lead to a repugnant outcome.

What rule of statutory interpretation has the judge used to interpret the statute?

A. The literal rule.
B. The mischief rule.

C. The parliamentary sovereignty rule.
D. The golden rule.
E. The purposive approach.

QUESTION 2

The High Court is considering a civil case concerning an employment law issue. The applicable section within the relevant statute is ambiguous. One of the parties claims that the minister responsible for introducing the legislation made clear statements about the meaning of the relevant section during parliamentary debates. The party claims that the statements clearly illustrate how Parliament intended the section to be applied to cases such as the one the court is hearing.

Which of the following statements most accurately describes whether the court may consult official records of the relevant parliamentary debates?

A. The court cannot refer to Hansard. All courts are prohibited from consulting Hansard because of the principle of parliamentary privilege.
B. The court may refer to Hansard as this is necessary to interpret the relevant statute.
C. The court may refer to Hansard if the relevant minister consents to the material being cited/used.
D. The court may consult Hansard if the relevant minister consents to waive parliamentary privilege.
E. The court may refer to Hansard because the relevant statute is ambiguous, and Hansard contains clear statements made by a minister as to the meaning of the section.

QUESTION 3

A court is considering a complex criminal law appeal. During the course of the case, various questions have arisen as to the precise meaning of a phrase contained within a statute. Both parties have put forward arguments regarding the correct interpretation of the phrase. A leading and highly respected academic in the field of criminal law has explored the relevant section of the statute extensively and has published articles on the matter. The judges hearing the case feel it would be useful to refer to the relevant articles to assist in construing the relevant section of the statute.

Which of the following statements most accurately describes the extent to which the court can use such external aids to assist in interpreting the statute?

A. The court may refer to external aids such as academic writings as the statute is unclear. In this case, the court may refer to the academic articles to assist in interpreting the relevant legislation.

B. The court may refer to external aids such as academic writings if it wishes to. In this case, the court may refer to the academic writings to assist in interpreting the relevant legislation.

C. The court may refer to external aids such as academic writings if both parties agree and the court feel it would assist in interpreting the relevant provision.

D. The court may not refer to academic writings since they are not parliamentary publications.

E. The court may refer to external aids as the statute is unclear. However, academic writings are not recognised as external aids to statutory interpretation.

QUESTION 4

A judge is considering a criminal law case. The defendant is charged with driving a vehicle on a public footpath contrary to an Act of Parliament. The relevant provision within the statute states that 'it is an offence to drive a car, motorcycle or any other motor-powered vehicle on a public footpath'. The defendant argues that he cannot be guilty of this offence as he was driving an electric scooter.

Which of the following statements most accurately describes the likely outcome should the judge apply the literal rule/approach?

A. A literal interpretation of the section would likely include electric scooters. The ordinary meaning of the term 'vehicle' would likely include scooters.

B. A literal interpretation of the section would likely exclude electric scooters. The ordinary and plain meaning of the term 'vehicle' would probably not include reference to scooters.

C. A literal interpretation of the section would likely include electric scooters. The Act is designed to ensure footpaths are safe for pedestrians so the court would interpret the section in accordance with Parliament's intention.
D. A literal interpretation of the section would likely exclude electric scooters. The statute specifically lists motor-powered vehicles. The electric scooter is not 'motor-powered' and would not be classified as a 'vehicle'.
E. A literal interpretation of the section would likely include electric scooters. The statute is designed to ensure that footpaths are safe for pedestrians. It is clear that any power-driven vehicle would pose a risk to pedestrians. The court would include electric-powered vehicles within the definition of a 'motor-powered vehicle'.

QUESTION 5

Parliament has recently passed legislation that criminalises the sale and distribution of a new and dangerous drug.

Which of the following statements most accurately describes the presumptions that a court would presume are implied in the statute?

A. The court would presume that the statute does not apply retrospectively and that any criminal offences stated in the statute require proof of mens rea (intention).
B. The court would presume that the statute does not apply retrospectively, and that any criminal offences require proof of mens rea unless the statute expressly states otherwise.
C. The court would presume that the statute does not apply retrospectively and comes into force on the stated commencement date.
D. The court would presume that any criminal offences stated in the statute require proof of mens rea (intention) unless the statute implies otherwise.
E. The court would presume that the statute alters any relevant pre-existing common law.

■ ANSWERS TO QUESTIONS

Answers to 'What do you know already?' questions at the start of the chapter

1) False. The courts *may* apply a purposive approach to statutory interpretation where a statute is unclear or ambiguous and the application of the other rules would result in an outcome that was absurd or repugnant or would clearly be inconsistent with the will of Parliament.
2) The following are internal/intrinsic aids to statutory interpretation:
   - long title
   - schedules within a statute.
3) The courts will always apply the literal rule first.
4) False. The rule in *Pepper v Hart relaxed* the rule that restricted courts from consulting Hansard to assist with statutory interpretation. The case lays out the circumstances in which Hansard can be used as an external aid to statutory interpretation.
5) In the case of *Smith v Hughes* [1960] 1 WLR 830 the courts applied the mischief rule.

Answers to end-of-chapter practice SQE1-style questions

Question 1:

The correct answer was D. The courts apply the golden rule where application of the literal rule would lead to a result that is 'absurd' or 'repugnant' (option A is therefore wrong). The mischief rule and purposive approach are used to understand the intention of Parliament (therefore options B and E are wrong). Option C is wrong as no such rule exists.

Question 2:

The correct answer was E. The court may refer to Hansard in cases where the relevant statute is ambiguous or obscure, and where the material from Hansard contains clear statements that were made by a minister regarding the meaning or scope of the relevant statute (therefore option A is incorrect). These criteria are satisfied in the scenario. The references to consent and parliamentary privilege are merely distractors and are not a requirement (therefore options C and D are incorrect). Option B is wrong because it is not sufficiently precise as to the circumstances when Hansard may be used.

Question 3:

The correct answer was A. Academic writings can be used as external/extrinsic aids to statutory interpretation (therefore option D is wrong). They can *only* be used where the statute is unclear or ambiguous (therefore option B is wrong). The scenario facts confirm that the statute is unclear and that the use of academic articles written by a well-respected academic would aid statutory interpretation. Option C is wrong as the consent of both parties is not required, and option E is wrong because the academic writings are treated as external aids.

Question 4:

The correct answer was D. A literal interpretation of the section would likely exclude electric scooters (therefore option A is wrong). Remember that the question required you to apply a literal interpretation of the words used. The statute specifically lists motor-powered vehicles. The electric scooter is not 'motor-powered' and probably would not be classified as a 'vehicle' either. Option B is wrong because it does not deal with the issue of 'motor-powered'. The literal rule requires that the words are given their ordinary and natural meaning. The court would not take into account the purpose of the statute if they applied the literal rule (therefore options C and E are wrong). Make sure you read the question carefully. The answer to this question would have been different if it asked you to determine the likely outcome if a different rule of statutory interpretation had been applied.

Question 5:

The correct answer was B. The courts always presume that certain things are implied in all statutes. These presumptions are only rebutted if the legislation *expressly* states otherwise. In the example given, courts would presume that the statute does not apply retrospectively, and that any criminal offences require proof of mens rea unless the statute *expressly* states otherwise. Remember that you have to select the single best answer. Other options in this question were factually accurate but were not the single 'best' answer.

■ KEY CASES, RULES, STATUTES AND INSTRUMENTS

The SQE1 Assessment Specification does not require you to know any case names, or statutory materials, for this topic. You are, however, expected to be familiar with the legal principles and rules outlined in the chapter.

4

Sources of law: case law

MAKE SURE YOU KNOW

In England and Wales, the two main sources of law are *legislation* and *case law*. Legislation is passed by Parliament and is the most authoritative source of law. A significant proportion of legislation is *primary* legislation contained within statutes. This chapter focuses on *case law*. In some cases, judges must decide *how to interpret the law* and *how to apply it* to the case facts before them. Such cases establish new legal principles or develop existing legal principles. When this happens, the decision sets a legal *precedent* and the case is reported in a *law report*. These legal precedents form a body of law known as *case law*. There are rules that help to ensure that case law is applied consistently by the various courts within the legal system. These rules *require* certain courts to follow precedents set by other courts within the court hierarchy. This system is known as the doctrine of *judicial precedent*. It is essential that you, an aspiring legal practitioner, understand what case law is and how judicial precedent operates.

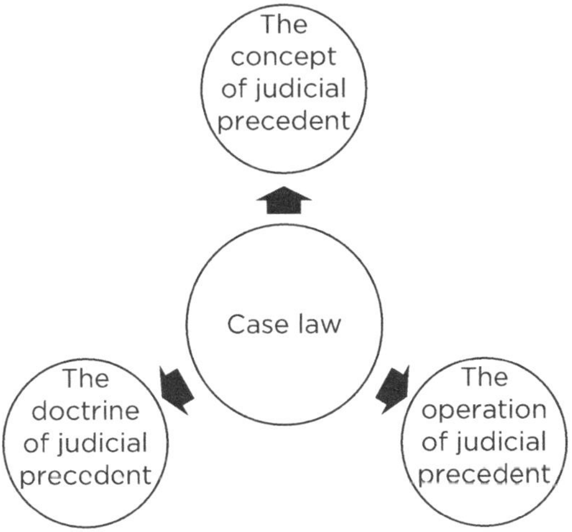

■ SQE ASSESSMENT ADVICE

For the SQE, you are required to understand the general principles that underpin the operation of judicial precedent. To understand how judicial precedent operates, you will need to understand what case law is and be able to identify which parts of a judgment form a binding precedent. You will also need to be able to distinguish between a *binding* precedent and a *persuasive* precedent and understand the circumstances in which different courts within the court hierarchy are bound to follow a precedent. In the SQE, it is likely that you will be required to apply the principles of judicial precedent to problem-based scenarios.

As you work through this chapter, remember to pay particular attention in your revision to:

- the principle of *stare decisis* and the doctrine of judicial precedent
- the general principles governing the operation of judicial precedent
- the circumstances in which courts are bound to follow or consider legal precedents set by other courts.

■ WHAT DO YOU KNOW ALREADY?

1) True or false: as the highest court in the UK, the Supreme Court is not bound by its own previous decisions. This ensures that the Supreme Court can alter the law as and when it is desirable to do so.

   [The operation of precedent, page 73]

2) In what circumstances may the Court of Appeal depart from its own decisions?

   [The operation of precedent, page 73]

3) Inferior courts are bound to follow the previous decisions of superior courts. However, inferior courts may avoid applying a binding precedent in certain circumstances. Explain the circumstances in which an inferior court may avoid applying a binding precedent.

   [The operation of precedent, page 73]

4) True or false: the Supreme Court is bound to follow the decisions of the European Court of Human Rights.

   [The operation of precedent, page 73]

5) Explain what is meant by the following terms:

   a) *ratio decidendi*

   b) *obiter dicta*

   c) binding precedent

   d) persuasive precedent.

   [The doctrine of judicial precedent, page 71]

THE DOCTRINE OF JUDICIAL PRECEDENT: GENERAL PRINCIPLES

Generally, when judges hear cases their role is to establish the facts of the case and apply the law to those facts. In many cases, the relevant law is clear and can be easily applied to a case. In other cases, judges will consider legal arguments relating to the *interpretation* of the law and *how it ought to apply* to the case facts. These legal arguments are typically formulated and advanced by the legal representatives of the parties to a case. The judge(s) will then determine what the law is and how it ought to be applied to the case facts before them. Senior appellate courts hear cases that are focused on questions of law *only*. Put simply, this means they hear cases that are concerned with the correct *interpretation* and *application* of the law. It is also important to remember that some areas of law developed through the historic common law system and have not been subject to legislative reform. The substantive law in those areas is therefore stated in, and developed through, case law. Where a judicial decision establishes or develops a legal principle or makes a statement of law, it creates a **precedent**. Collectively, these precedents form a body of law known as **case law**.

Key term: precedent

In law, the term 'precedent' refers to a previous judicial decision that established, developed, modified or clarified a legal principle or statement of the law. Precedents are often referred to legal authorities.

Key term: case law

The term 'case law' refers to the body of judge-made law that derives from judicial decisions in past cases. Case law is comprised of legal principles and rules that have either a binding or persuasive effect on subsequent cases.

When a case sets a precedent, it is reported in a law report. The decision of the court is recorded and explained, often in great detail, in the judgment(s) to the case. Judgments contain what is commonly referred to as the 'ratio' of the case. This derives from the Latin term '*ratio decidendi*', which means 'the reason for the decision'. The ratio includes the statement(s) of law and the explanation of why the court reached that decision. Any other statements within the judgment are known as *obiter dicta*. This means 'other things said'. These comments are, in essence, *supplementary* to the decision rather than *part of* the decision.

It is important to note that *only* the *ratio decidendi* parts of a judgment form a binding legal precedent. Unfortunately, judgments are not neatly split into sections that outline the legal decision, the *ratio decidendi* and the *obiter dicta*. As an aspiring solicitor, it is important that you develop the ability to identify and extrapolate the binding part(s) of judgments. It is also important that you understand that precedents may be binding or persuasive, as shown in **Figure 4.1**.

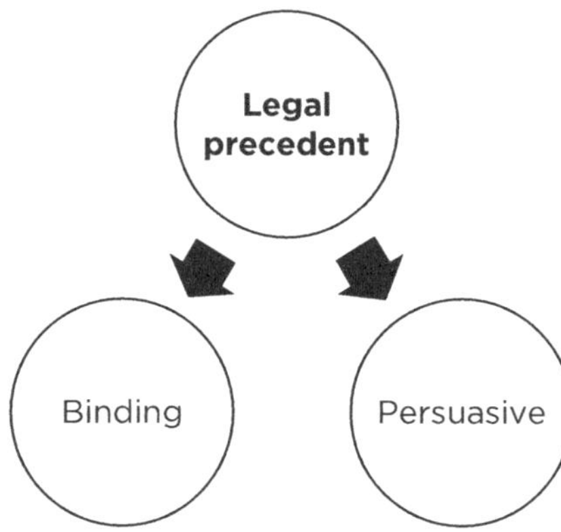

Figure 4.1: Legal precedent

A **binding precedent** is one that *must* be followed by other courts in future cases. This is because binding precedents are subject to the principle of ***stare decisis***. This principle derives from a Latin maxim meaning to 'stand by previous decisions'. Put simply, the principle dictates that judges should interpret and apply the law consistently in cases where the case facts and/or issues are the same or similar to previous cases, and thus they should **follow** previous judicial decisions where possible.

Key term: binding precedent

The term 'binding precedent' refers to a legal precedent that must be followed by other courts in future cases. In England and Wales, a court is bound to follow precedents set by the courts that sit above it in the court hierarchy.

Key term: *stare decisis*

The principle of *stare decisis* requires that previous decisions are followed by courts in subsequent cases with similar facts and legal issues. The principle is designed to promote certainty and consistency in the application of the law.

Courts are *not bound* to follow a **persuasive precedent**, but they *may* take it into account, and it may *influence* the decision of a court in a future case.

> **Key term: persuasive precedent**
>
> A persuasive precedent refers to a legal precedent that a court *may* rely on in reaching a decision in future cases. For example, a precedent may be *persuasive* because the case is from a different jurisdiction.

This system of applying previous judicial decisions to decide future cases is known as the **doctrine of judicial precedent**.

> **Key term: doctrine of judicial precedent**
>
> The doctrine of judicial precedent is underpinned by the principle of *stare decisis*, which requires courts to follow previous decisions in order to promote the consistent application of the law. The phrase 'doctrine of judicial precedent' refers to the principles that govern the way that precedent operates.

THE OPERATION OF PRECEDENT

The operation of judicial precedent is directly linked to the court hierarchy. **Figure 4.2** outlines the core principles that underpin the operation of judicial precedent. Make sure that you learn these general principles!

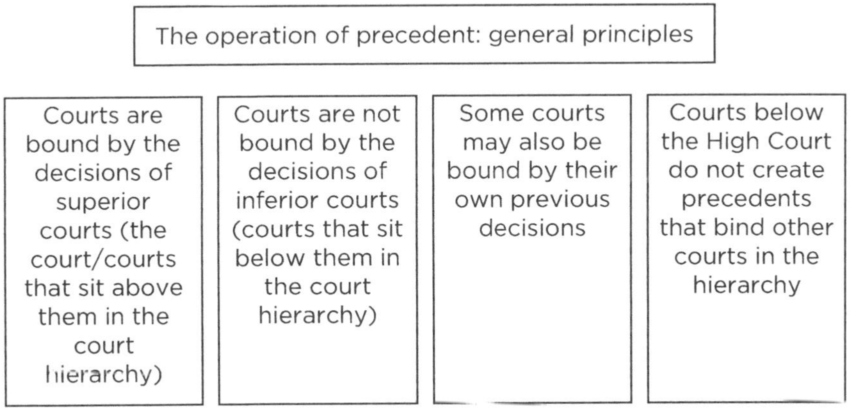

Figure 4.2: The operation of precedent: general principles

Revision tip

It is important that you understand the court hierarchy. You may find it useful to read **Chapter 1** of this revision guide in order to remind yourself of where each court sits in the court hierarchy.

Precedent and the court hierarchy

Precedents are set by the senior courts within the court hierarchy. The meaning of the term senior courts is discussed in **Chapter 1, page 8**. Specifically, precedents are set by the Supreme Court, the Court of Appeal and the High Court. This is because these courts usually consider cases concerning questions of law (eg how the law should be interpreted or applied).

The Supreme Court is the highest court in the UK. As such, it hears cases that concern points of law of general public importance. Its decisions bind *all* other courts in the court hierarchy. It is typically bound by its own decisions (and by decisions of its predecessor, the House of Lords). It is permitted 'to depart from a previous decision when it appears right to do so', but it rarely exercises this power.

The Court of Appeal considers appeal cases concerning questions of law. It is bound by the decisions of the Supreme Court. It binds all other courts in the court hierarchy and is generally bound by its own decisions, although the Civil Division and Criminal Division do not bind each other. It may depart from an existing Court of Appeal decision *only* where one of the exceptions in *Young v Bristol Aeroplane Co Ltd* [1944] KB 718 (CA) apply. The exceptions are as follows:

- Where there are two conflicting decisions of the Court of Appeal, it may choose which precedent to follow.
- Where a previous decision of the Court of Appeal has been expressly or impliedly overruled by a Supreme Court decision, it must follow the Supreme Court precedent.
- The Court of Appeal is not bound by a previous decision where it is deemed to have been made *per incuriam*. Put simply, a case may be considered to have been made *per incuriam* if the court failed, through lack of care, to apply a relevant statutory provision or a binding precedent when making a decision and this resulted in the court making a decision that would have been different had the relevant legal authority/authorities been applied. Such cases are rare.

Exam warning

In the SQE, it is likely that you will be required to demonstrate that you know the circumstances in which the various courts in the court hierarchy are bound to follow the decisions of other courts and/or their own previous decisions. Remember that the principle of precedent is essential to the coherent development of the law. Consequently, courts are bound to follow the decisions of courts above them in the court hierarchy, and higher courts are generally bound by their own precedents. Higher courts may *only* depart from their previous decisions where a prescribed exception exists. **Table 4.1** summarises the key points to remember.

Table 4.1: Precedent: key revision points to revise ahead of the SQE

Court	Key revision points
Supreme Court	• It binds all other courts in the court hierarchy. • It is typically bound by its own decisions (and by decisions of its predecessor, the House of Lords). • It may depart from a previous decision when it appears right to do so but it rarely exercises this power. There must be a compelling reason to depart from its own decisions.
Judicial Committee of the Privy Council (JCPC)	• Decisions of the JCPC are *not* binding on domestic courts. • Its decisions are persuasive rather than binding. • Its decisions are typically followed by domestic courts.
Court of Appeal (Civil Division)	• The Court of Appeal (Civil Division) is bound by the Supreme Court. • Its decisions are binding on all courts lower than it in the court hierarchy. • Its decisions do not bind the Court of Appeal (Criminal Division). • The Civil Division is usually bound by its own decisions, but it can depart from previous decisions if any of the exceptions laid out in *Young v Bristol Aeroplane Co Ltd* [1944] KB 718 (CA) apply.
Court of Appeal (Criminal Division)	• The Court of Appeal (Criminal Division) is bound by the Supreme Court. • Its decisions are binding on all courts lower than it in the court hierarchy. • Its decisions do not bind the Court of Appeal (Civil Division). • The Criminal Division is usually bound by its own decisions, but it can depart from previous decisions if any of the *Young v Bristol Aeroplane Co Ltd* [1944] KB 718 (CA) exceptions apply.

Table 4.1: Continued

Court	Key revision points
Court of Appeal (Criminal Division)	• *Additionally*, because it deals with criminal cases that are likely to impact an individual's liberty, the Criminal Division may depart from its previous decisions 'where the liberty of an individual is at stake'. The Criminal Division has a wider power to disapply a precedent than the Civil Division.
High Court	• When the High Court is exercising its appellate jurisdiction (considering an appeal case) it is bound by the Supreme Court, the Court of Appeal and its own decisions (unless one of the exceptions laid out in *Young v Bristol Aeroplane Co Ltd* [1944] KB 718 (CA) applies). • When the High Court is exercising its supervisory jurisdiction (considering a judicial review case) it is bound by the Supreme Court and the Court of Appeal. It is not, however, bound by its own decisions. The power to depart from its own decisions is rarely exercised. • When the High Court is hearing a case at first instance, it is bound by the Supreme Court, the Court of Appeal and the High Court Divisional Courts. • Decisions of the High Court are binding on courts below it in the court hierarchy.
Crown Court	• The Crown Court is bound by decisions of the Court of Appeal and the Supreme Court. • While the Crown Court is classed as a senior court, its decisions do not bind any other court. • The Crown Court is not bound by its previous decisions, but its previous decisions may be very persuasive.
Courts of first instance: magistrates' court, County Court and Family Court	• These 'inferior' courts are bound by the decisions of all superior courts. • These courts do not bind themselves and do not create precedents. • The Family Court is staffed by various members of the judiciary. The decisions of more senior judges sitting in the Family Court create precedents that must be followed by lower-ranked judges sitting in the Family Court.

If you are asked to determine whether a court is bound to follow a precedent set by another court, you may find it useful to work through the decision tree shown in **Figure 4.3**. You can then test your ability to apply your knowledge to a practice-based scenario in **Practice example 4.1**.

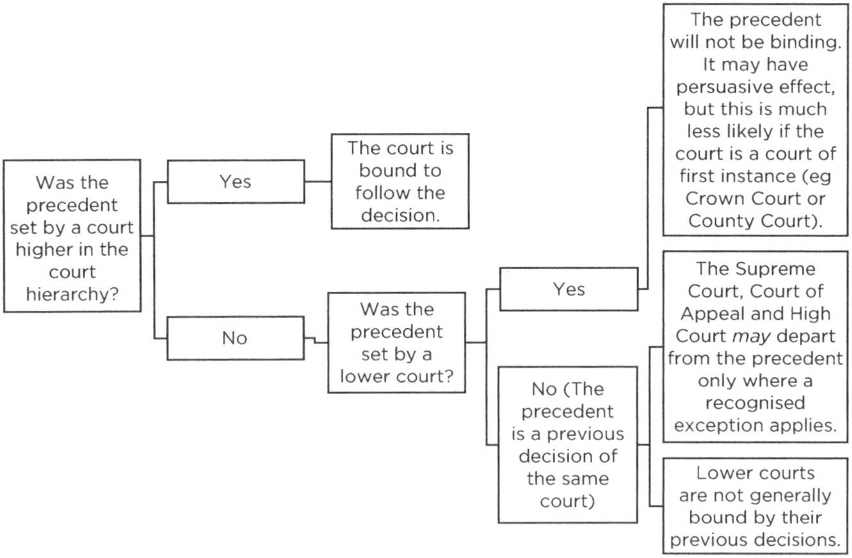

Figure 4.3: Precedent decision tree

Practice example 4.1

The Court of Appeal is considering a civil appeal. The appellant's submissions rely on a previous decision of the Court of Appeal (Civil Division) which indicates that the appeal should be allowed. The respondent's submissions rely on a previous decision of the Court of Appeal (Civil Division) which indicates that the appeal should not be allowed.

How should the Court of Appeal treat the two decisions to which it has been referred?

The Court of Appeal is generally bound to follow its own previous decisions. However, here it appears that there are two conflicting Court of Appeal decisions. This is a recognised exception as per *Young v Bristol Aeroplane Co Ltd* [1944] KB 718 (CA) so the Court of Appeal may choose which precedent to follow.

Precedent and European courts

The Human Rights Act 1998 requires all courts in England and Wales to take into account decisions of the European Court of Human Rights. Courts are not bound to follow its decisions, but precedents set by the European Court of Human Rights are persuasive. This position was *not* impacted by the European Union (Withdrawal) Act 2018.

The relationship between domestic courts and the Court of Justice of the European Union (CJEU) was fundamentally altered by the European Union (Withdrawal) Act 2018 (and related legislation). The courts of England and Wales are not bound to follow decisions of the CJEU.

Revision tip

For the SQE1 assessments, you will need to understand the place of EU law in the UK constitution. Furthermore you need to know about the European Convention on Human Rights and the Human Rights Act 1998. These topics are covered in detail in ***Revise SQE: Constitutional and Administrative and EU Law***, Chapters 9 and 8.

THE OPERATION OF JUDICIAL PRECEDENT: DEALING WITH PRECEDENTS

It is important to remember that no two cases are the same. Case facts and issues may be similar, but the specific facts and issues in each case will differ from past cases. In practical terms, this means that judges sometimes have to decide whether to apply a precedent to the case before them. Courts must follow a precedent if the material facts of the case are the same or similar to a previous decision. When it does this, the court is said to **follow** the binding precedent.

Key term: follow

In the context of the doctrine of judicial precedent, the term 'follow' is used to describe the application of a binding legal precedent to a case. For example, the Court of Appeal *followed* the House of Lords decision in *R v Wood*.

If an appellate court is considering an appeal against a lower court's decision, it may **reverse** the decision of the lower court. A court may reverse a decision where it feels that the lower court's interpretation or application of the law was incorrect. This is because appeals are considered by more senior courts/judges and so the decision of the appellate court 'trumps' the decision reached by the lower court. When a court reverses a decision, it creates a new precedent that must be followed in future cases (subject to the usual rules of precedent outlined above).

Key term: reverse

In the context of the doctrine of judicial precedent, the term 'reverse' is used to describe the outcome of an appeal where the appellate court determines that the lower court's decision was wrong. For example, the Court of Appeal considered an appeal from the Crown Court and *reversed* the decision.

It is important to note that reversing a lower court's decision is not the same as overruling a precedent. Superior courts may **overrule** a precedent where they feel that the previous decision is wrong or no longer an accurate representation of the law. For example, the Supreme Court may overrule a long-standing precedent set by its predecessor, the House of Lords. The key point to remember is that overruling is *only* possible within the bounds of the doctrine of judicial precedent more generally. For example, it is not possible for a lower court to overrule the decision of a higher court. Similarly, the Court of Appeal cannot overrule its own decisions unless one of the *Young v Bristol Aeroplane Co Ltd* [1944] exceptions apply.

Key term: overrule

In the context of the doctrine of judicial precedent, the term 'overrule' is used to describe a court's decision to declare that an existing precedent is wrong or no longer an accurate representation of the law. For example, the Supreme Court has the power to *overrule* precedents set by lower courts and may overrule its own decisions where it considers it right to do so.

A court may also **distinguish** a precedent where it feels the material facts of a case differ from the precedent and it is therefore not bound to follow the precedent. This means the precedent remains good law *and* the new decision sets a precedent. Sometimes, courts distinguish cases on the basis of very fine distinctions, and this causes incoherent case law. **Practice example 4.2** (overleaf) illustrates how this topic could be assessed in the SQE1 assessments.

Key term: distinguish

In the context of the doctrine of judicial precedent, the term 'distinguish' is used to describe circumstances where a court does not deem itself to be bound by an existing binding precedent because of material differences between the cases. For example, the High Court *distinguished* the Court of Appeal authority on the basis that the material facts were not sufficiently similar.

Practice example 4.2

The Supreme Court considers a complex appeal case. It determines that the Court of Appeal's decision was based on an incorrect interpretation of existing case law and therefore finds in favour of the appellant.

How has the Supreme Court treated the Court of Appeal's previous decision?

In this case, the Supreme Court is hearing an appeal from the Court of Appeal. It has reached a decision that differs from the Court of Appeal's decision because it found in favour of the party making the appeal (the appellants). The Supreme Court has therefore reversed the decision of the Court of Appeal.

■ KEY POINT CHECKLIST

- Case law is judge-made law that is created by virtue of judicial decisions in past cases.
- Some cases set precedents that must be followed by other courts in future cases.
- A case will typically set a precedent if the decision established, developed, modified or clarified a legal principle or statement of the law.
- Precedents may be binding or persuasive. A binding precedent *must* be followed in future cases where the case facts are sufficiently similar. Courts may choose to apply persuasive precedents but are not bound to follow them.
- The doctrine of precedent is underpinned by the principle of *stare decisis*. Put simply, the principle requires courts to follow existing precedents where the case facts and/or issues are the same or similar to previous cases.

- The operation of judicial precedent is directly linked to the court hierarchy. Binding precedents are set by the Supreme Court, the Court of Appeal and the High Court. In England and Wales, a court is bound to *follow* the decisions of any courts that sit above it in the court hierarchy.
- Courts that create binding precedent are bound to follow their own previous decisions. However, the Supreme Court may depart from its own decisions where it considers it right to do so, and the Court of Appeal and High Court may depart from its own previous decisions if any of the exemptions laid out in *Young v Bristol Aeroplane Co Ltd* [1944] KB 718 (CA) apply. In such cases, these courts may *overrule* an existing precedent.
- Lower courts do not generally create binding precedents and do not generally bind themselves. Lower courts must follow binding precedents set by higher courts.
- A court may decide to *distinguish* a precedent on the basis of material differences between the relevant cases.

KEY TERMS AND CONCEPTS

- precedent (**page 71**)
- case law (**page 71**)
- binding precedent (**page 72**)
- *stare decisis* (**page 72**)
- persuasive precedent (**page 73**)
- doctrine of judicial precedent (**page 73**)
- follow (**page 78**)
- reverse (**page 79**)
- overrule (**page 79**)
- distinguish (**page 80**)

SQE1-STYLE QUESTIONS

QUESTION 1

The Court of Appeal is considering a civil appeal. The appellant's submissions rely on a previous decision of the JCPC which indicates that the appeal should be allowed. The JCPC judgment did not indicate that the decision would be binding in England and Wales. The respondent's submissions rely on a previous decision of the Court of Appeal which indicates that the appeal should not be allowed.

How should the Court of Appeal treat the two decisions to which it has been referred?

A. The court should treat both previous decisions as having persuasive value only and must decide which of the two to follow.
B. The court should consider itself bound by the earlier decision of the Court of Appeal.
C. The court should consider itself bound by the earlier decision of the JCPC.
D. The court should consider itself bound by both decisions and must choose which of the two to follow.
E. The court should treat both earlier decisions as having persuasive value only and may choose whether to apply either precedent to the instant case.

QUESTION 2

In the [fictitious] case of *Jones v Morritt*, the Court of Appeal decided that the [fictitious] case *Smith v Hodgson* was wrongly decided and overruled the decision. *Smith v Hodgson* was decided by the Divisional Court (High Court).

Which of the following statements most accurately describes the status of Smith v Hodgson?

A. The effect of the Court of Appeal decision in *Jones v Morritt* is that *Smith v Hodgson* is now a persuasive precedent rather than a binding precedent.
B. The effect of the Court of Appeal decision in *Jones v Morritt* is that *Smith v Hodgson* remains good law and may be relied on in future cases.
C. The effect of the Court of Appeal decision in *Jones v Morritt* is that *Smith v Hodgson* remains a binding precedent on all inferior courts.
D. The effect of the Court of Appeal decision in *Jones v Morritt* is that *Smith v Hodgson* was distinguished and may be relied on in future cases.
E. The effect of the Court of Appeal decision in *Jones v Morritt* is that *Smith v Hodgson* is no longer good law.

QUESTION 3

In an appeal before the Supreme Court, the respondent relies on an earlier House of Lords decision that indicates that the Supreme Court should find in the respondent's favour. The appellant relies on more recent authorities from the Court of Appeal, which suggest that the Supreme Court should find in favour of the appellant.

Which of the following statements most accurately describes how the Supreme Court should treat the authorities to which it has been referred?

A. The court should consider itself bound by the earlier decision of the House of Lords.

B. The court should not consider itself to be bound by the decisions of its predecessor, the House of Lords, or the Court of Appeal decisions.

C. The court should consider itself bound by the most recent legal authority to which it has been referred.

D. The court should treat all authorities as having persuasive value only and must decide which of the authorities to follow.

E. The court should consider itself bound by the earlier decision of the House of Lords and may only depart from the decision if there are compelling reasons to do so.

QUESTION 4

The Court of Appeal (Criminal Division) is hearing a criminal appeal case concerning the interpretation of the phrase 'motor-powered vehicle'. The appellant submits that an electric-powered scooter ought to be regarded as a 'motor-powered vehicle'. In support of this submission, the appellant is relying on a previous Supreme Court decision. The [fictitious] Supreme Court case did not concern an electric-powered scooter but the leading judgment included the following statement: 'For the purposes of determining whether a vehicle falls within the scope of the Act, one must determine whether the vehicle in question is one which is mechanically propelled, rather than whether it is powered by a motor. If it is mechanically propelled, it is likely to fall within the statute'.

Which of the following statements most accurately describes the effect of the Supreme Court's statement?

A. The statement is a legally binding precedent that the Court of Appeal is bound to follow.

B. The statement is a legally binding precedent that the Court of Appeal may follow, distinguish or overrule.

C. The statement has persuasive effect only and the Court of Appeal may apply the precedent.
D. The statement has persuasive effect only but is likely to be highly influential because of the seniority of the Supreme Court.
E. The statement is a legally binding precedent, but the Court of Appeal may distinguish the case on the basis that the material facts are not the same as those in the present case.

QUESTION 5

The High Court hears an appeal concerning a contract law dispute. The case was first considered by the County Court. The High Court determines that the County Court's decision is wrong.

Which of the following most accurately describes the decision of the High Court?

A. Both the High Court and the County Court decisions would be considered legally binding on inferior courts.
B. The High Court has distinguished the previous decision of the County Court. Both the High Court and the County Court decisions would be considered legally binding on inferior courts.
C. The High Court has overruled the previous decision of the County Court.
D. The High Court decision reversed the County Court's decision. The High Court decision sets a new precedent that inferior courts are bound to follow in future cases.
E. The High Court decision reversed the County Court's decision. The High Court decision sets a new precedent that all courts are bound to follow in future cases.

■ ANSWERS TO QUESTIONS

Answers to 'What do you know already?' questions at the start of the chapter

1) False. The Supreme Court typically follows its own previous decisions. This ensures the law develops in a consistent and coherent manner.

2) The Court of Appeal may depart from its own decisions where one of the exceptions laid out in *Young v Bristol Aeroplane Co Ltd* [1944] KB 718 (CA) applies. The exceptions are as follows:
   - Where there are two conflicting Court of Appeal decisions, it may choose which to follow.
   - Where a previous decision of the Court of Appeal has been expressly or impliedly overruled by the Supreme Court it must follow the Supreme Court precedent.
   - The Court of Appeal is not bound where the previous decision is deemed to have been made *per incuriam*.
3) Inferior courts may avoid applying a binding precedent by *distinguishing* the precedent on the basis that the cases are not materially the same.
4) False. The Supreme Court must take the decisions of the European Court of Human Rights into account, but it is not bound to follow them.
5) Terms explained:
   - The term '*ratio decidendi*' means 'the reason for the decision'. It refers to the parts of a judgment that contain the statement(s) of law and an explanation of why the judge(s) reached that decision. This is the part of the decision that forms a binding precedent.
   - The term '*obiter dicta*' means 'other things said'. It refers to any comments within a judgment that are *supplementary* to the decision, rather than *part of* the decision in the case.
   - The term 'binding precedent' refers to a legal precedent that must be followed by other courts in future cases.
   - The term 'persuasive precedent' refers to a legal precedent that a court *may choose* to rely on in reaching a decision in future cases.

Answers to end-of-chapter SQE1-style questions

Question 1:

The correct answer was B. The Court of Appeal is bound to follow its own previous decisions (therefore options A and E are wrong). Its previous decisions are not merely persuasive. The Court of Appeal may only depart from its previous decisions in limited circumstances, which do not apply here. The decisions of the JCPC are usually persuasive only (therefore options C and D are wrong).

Question 2:

The correct answer was E. The Court of Appeal *overruled* the decision in *Smith v Hodgson*. Where a court overrules a precedent, that precedent ceases to be good law. Options A, B, C and D state that *Smith v Hodgson* will continue to have a binding or persuasive effect on future cases, and so cannot be correct.

Question 3:

The correct answer was E. Previous decisions of the House of Lords bind the Supreme Court (therefore option B is wrong). The Supreme Court does, however, have the power to depart from an existing precedent where there are compelling reasons to do so (therefore option A is wrong). This means that option E is the most accurate description of the Supreme Court's position. Option C is incorrect as the Supreme Court is only bound by itself, and no other court. Option D is wrong because the Supreme Court cannot treat its own previous decision as persuasive.

Question 4:

The correct answer was D. The statement made is likely to be considered *obiter dicta* and thus is not binding (therefore options A, B and E are incorrect). It does not specifically deal with whether an electric scooter falls with s1(2). *Obiter dicta* statements made by the Supreme Court are likely to be very persuasive to lower courts, such as the Court of Appeal. Option C is incorrect because it is not as accurate as option D.

Question 5:

The correct answer was D. The High Court has considered an appeal and reversed the County Court decision. Option E is incorrect because it states that the new precedent binds all other courts. High Court decisions *only* bind courts below it in the court hierarchy. Option C is wrong because the High Court has not *overruled* a decision; it has *reversed* it. Options A and B are incorrect because the County Court decision would not be legally binding.

■ KEY CASES, RULES, STATUTES AND INSTRUMENTS

The SQE1 Assessment Specification does not require you to know any case names, or statutory materials, for this topic. You are, however, expected to be familiar with the legal principles and rules outlined in the chapter.

5

The regulation of legal services

■ MAKE SURE YOU KNOW

You may be surprised to learn that a range of professionals can provide legal services. However, certain 'reserved' activities may only be carried out by those with appropriate authorisation. Those who are authorised to carry on such activities are subject to regulation. For the SQE1 assessments, you need to know which *regulated* legal service providers may operate in England and Wales and which bodies regulate such providers. Solicitors form the largest group of legal service providers and are regulated by the Solicitors Regulation Authority (SRA). This chapter provides an overview of the SRA's regulatory role and outlines the key aspects of regulation that you need to know for the SQE.

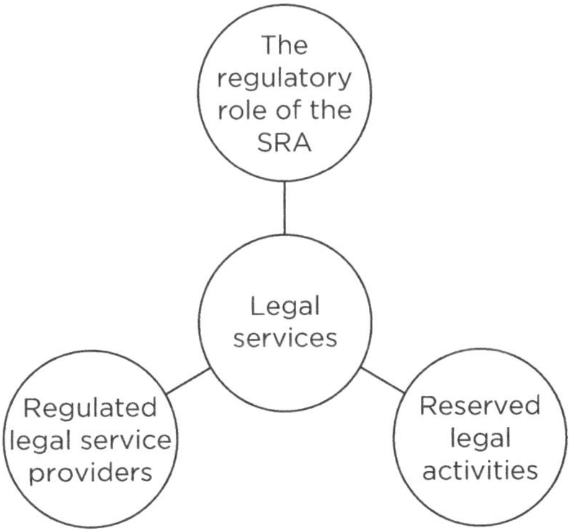

SQE ASSESSMENT ADVICE

For the SQE, you are required to know about the regulation of legal service providers. In particular, you need to understand the regulatory role of the SRA.

As you work through this chapter, remember to pay particular attention in your revision to:

- 'reserved legal activities'
- other regulated providers of legal services
- the regulatory role of the SRA
- the seven fundamental principles
- the concept of 'risk-based regulation'
- professional indemnity insurance.

WHAT DO YOU KNOW ALREADY?

Have a go at these questions before reading this chapter. If you find some difficult or cannot remember the answers, make a note to look more closely at that during your revision.

1) True or false: all legal service providers are regulated by the SRA.
   [Regulated legal service providers, page 91]
2) Which of the following are classified as 'reserved legal activities'?
   - drafting a will
   - issuing a civil claim in the County Court
   - appearing in the Crown Court on behalf of a client
   - drafting probate papers
   - administering an oath.

   [Reserved legal activities, page 89]
3) What is professional indemnity insurance?
   [Professional indemnity insurance, page 100]
4) List the seven fundamental principles set out in the SRA Standards and Regulations.
   [Principles, page 97]
5) Explain what is meant by the term 'risk-based regulation'.
   [Risk-based regulation, page 98]

LEGAL SERVICES IN ENGLAND AND WALES

There is no set definition of the term 'legal services'. It is an umbrella term that includes advice, help and representation relating to legal matters. As you might imagine, it covers a wide array of activities, from drafting a multi-million-pound contract to drafting a basic will. The framework for the regulation of legal services is laid out in the Legal Services Act 2007 (LSA). Although you are not required to know the LSA for the purposes of SQE1, it is worth familiarising yourself with its key provisions.

Reserved legal activities

In the past, a significant proportion of legal work could only be carried out by solicitors or barristers. As a result of changes to the legal services market, other providers may now provide legal services. However, certain 'reserved' legal activities can *only* be carried out by those who are authorised or exempt from requiring authorisation. The LSA distinguishes between those legal services that are classified as **reserved legal activities** and those that are not. It is essential that you understand which activities are classified as 'reserved' because reserved legal activities can *only* be provided by authorised persons. Those authorised to engage in reserved legal activities are subject to regulation.

Key term: reserved legal activities

The term 'reserved legal activities' refers to the aspects of legal practice that only a suitably qualified legal professional is permitted to carry out by virtue of the LSA 2007. Reserved legal activities are listed in s 12 of the Act.

Carrying out a 'reserved legal activity' without appropriate authorisation constitutes a criminal offence. Section 12 outlines the six categories of reserved legal activities – these are outlined in **Table 5.1**.

Table 5.1: Reserved legal activities

Reserved legal activity	Overview
s 12(1)(a) the exercise of a right of audience	This refers to the right to appear before and address a court. This includes the right to call and examine witnesses.

Table 5.1: Continued

Reserved legal activity	Overview
s 12(1)(b) the conduct of litigation	Conduct of litigation includes: • *issuing proceedings* before any court in England and Wales • *commencing, prosecuting or defending such proceedings* • carrying out ancillary tasks associated with such proceedings.
s 12(1)(c) reserved instrument activities	Reserved instrument activities are those that involve preparing or lodging certain legal instruments (formal legal documents). Reserved instrument activities are those dealing with the transfer, charge or registration of land under the Land Registration Act 2002, or any other legal instrument relating to real or personal estate for the purposes of the law of England and Wales, or any instrument relating to court proceedings in England and Wales. It is important to note that the preparation of some types of documents are *not* classified as reserved instrument activities. Examples include: • drafting wills and other testamentary instruments • drafting agreements not intended to be executed as a deed • drafting a letter or power of attorney.
s 12(1)(d) probate activities	Probate activities include: • preparing the documents needed to obtain a grant of probate • preparing a grant of letters of administration • preparing documents to oppose a grant of probate/grant of letters of administration.
s 12(1)(e) notarial activities	Notarial activities involve certifying and authenticating certain documents. Here, the term refers to any activities that were previously carried on by notaries in accordance with the Public Notaries Act 1801.
s 12(1)(f) the administration of oaths	This refers to the power to administer an oath (eg taking oaths and swearing affidavits)

Only the activities outlined in s 12 are classified as 'reserved'. All other legal activities are, by default, 'non-reserved' activities. Non-reserved activities can be provided by unregulated individuals without a formal requirement for training or qualifications. Some common examples of non-reserved legal activities include will writing, providing legal advice and providing mediation services. Test your ability to differentiate between reserved and non-reserved activities by answering **Practice example 5.1**.

Practice example 5.1

A client is seeking advice regarding divorce procedure. While the client is entitled to complete the divorce documentation himself, he would prefer for 'a professional' to deal with the completion and submission of the relevant court documents. Are any of these activities 'reserved' activities under s 12?

The giving of legal advice is not a reserved legal activity. However, completing formal court documents *and* submitting them on behalf of the client would constitute reserved legal activities.

Regulated legal service providers

As noted above, there are a number of regulated legal service providers. Consequently, there are also a number of approved regulatory bodies who regulate legal service providers. Each regulatory body is linked to a specific profession or specialism. The Legal Services Board (LSB) is responsible for overseeing and monitoring these regulators. Authorisation to carry on reserved legal activities must be obtained from the relevant regulator (s 18). The different regulated legal service providers and corresponding regulatory bodies are listed in **Table 5.2**.

Table 5.2: Regulated legal services providers and regulatory bodies

Regulated legal service provider	Relevant regulatory body	Overview of regulator's authorisation powers
Solicitors	Solicitors Regulation Authority (SRA)	It can authorise solicitors and firms to carry out 'reserved legal activities', except notarial activities.
Barristers	Bar Standards Board (BSB)	It can authorise barristers to provide all types of reserved legal activity, except notarial activities.

Table 5.2: Continued

Regulated legal service provider	Relevant regulatory body	Overview of regulator's authorisation powers
Chartered legal executives	CILEx Regulation	It can authorise chartered legal executives to provide all types of reserved legal activity, except notarial activities.
Licensed conveyancers	Council for Licensed Conveyancers	It can authorise licensed conveyancers to conduct reserved instrument activities, probate activities and the administration of oaths.
Patent attorneys/ agents	Intellectual Property Regulation Board	It can authorise patent attorneys to conduct all reserved legal activity except probate and notarial activities.
Trademark attorneys	Intellectual Property Regulation Board	It can authorise trademark attorneys to conduct all reserved legal activity except probate and notarial activities.
Costs lawyers	Costs Lawyers Standards Board	It can authorise costs lawyers to exercise rights of audience, conduct litigation and administer oaths.
Notaries	Master of the Faculties	It can authorise notaries to carry out all reserved legal activities except exercising rights of audience and conducting litigation. The Master of Faculties is the *only* regulator that can authorise notarial activities.
Chartered accountants	Institute of Chartered Accountants in England and Wales	The Institute of Chartered Accountants may authorise chartered accountants to carry out probate activities.

It is important to note that an authorised person is subject to the regulatory requirements of the relevant approved regulator. For example, solicitors are subject to the regulation of the SRA, chartered legal executives are regulated by CILEx Regulation and so on and so forth. It is also important to note that regulation extends to *all* legal services the authorised person carries out, not just those services classified as reserved legal activities. So, a solicitor must comply with the SRA's regulations and codes of conduct even where they are not carrying out reserved legal activities. For example, a solicitor drafting a will for a client must adhere to SRA's regulations and codes of conduct even though will writing is not a reserved legal activity.

Exemption

Section 19 states that a person is exempt from requiring authorisation if they are defined as exempt in Schedule 3 of the LSA. For example, a person may exercise rights of audience if a specific court has granted that person a right of audience in respect of specific proceedings. Similarly, a person may engage in the conduct of litigation if they have been granted a right to conduct litigation by a specific court. Courts may grant such rights where they are empowered to do so by virtue of a particular statutory provision. A person may also be exempt because they are a party to the proceedings or because they are acting as a McKenzie Friend.

Revision tip

Remember a person is not required to be authorised or exempt to engage in non-reserved legal activities that fall outside the scope of s 12.

THE REGULATORY ROLE OF THE SRA

The SRA is the independent regulatory arm of the Law Society of England and Wales. The SRA regulates solicitors and law firms in England and Wales (in this book, reference to the term 'solicitor' includes registered European lawyers and registered foreign lawyers). The SQE will assess your knowledge and understanding of the regulatory aspects of the SRA's work. In its regulatory capacity, the SRA is responsible for:

- licensing individuals *and* firms to practise
- setting the standards of the profession
- enforcing compliance against those standards.

Solicitors are specialists who provide legal services. They may work in law firms, in government, in the justice system or within companies. Some law firms are enormous whereas others are single-solicitor practices. Because the profession is diverse, the day-to-day work undertaken by solicitors is very wide-ranging. However, it is important to remember that *all* solicitors must abide by the same professional principles and codes of conduct. These principles and codes of conduct are set by the SRA and are contained within the SRA Standards and Regulations. A solicitor who does not comply with the SRA Standards and Regulations may face disciplinary action by the SRA.

SRA authorisation

As an approved regulator, the SRA is responsible for authorising individuals and firms to carry on legal activities (see **Figure 5.1**).

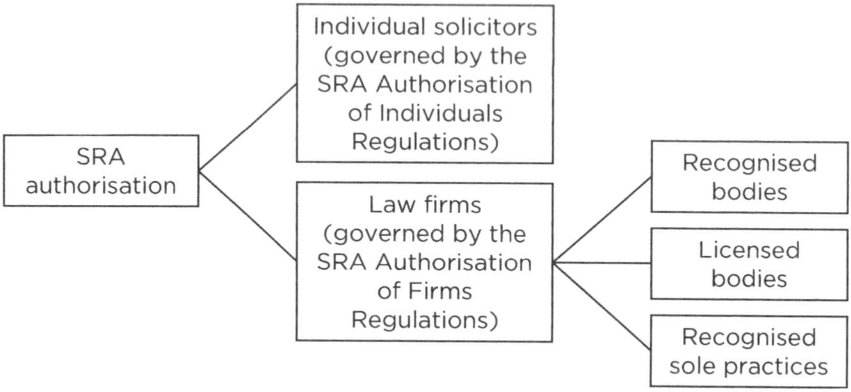

Figure 5.1: SRA authorisation

Authorisation of solicitors

To be able to practise as a solicitor, a person must satisfy the three requirements laid out in s 1 of the Solicitors Act 1974. These are summarised in **Figure 5.2**.

Revision tip

Remember that while solicitors have rights of audience, they cannot exercise those rights in the higher courts unless they successfully complete additional advocacy qualifications (this is discussed in **Chapter 1**, **rights of audience**).

Carrying on reserved legal activities

Practising certificates are personal to individual solicitors. The certificate authorises a solicitor to carry on all reserved legal activities (except notarial activities). However, it is important to remember that reserved legal activities must ordinarily be provided through an authorised entity (such as a law firm). Therefore, generally speaking, solicitors must hold a valid practising certificate *and* carry on all reserved legal activities through an authorised body.

There are some exceptions to this general rule. For example, some solicitors work on a freelance basis. Typically, freelance solicitors have to be authorised as a recognised sole practice. However, a freelance solicitor is *not* required to be authorised as a recognised sole practice where their

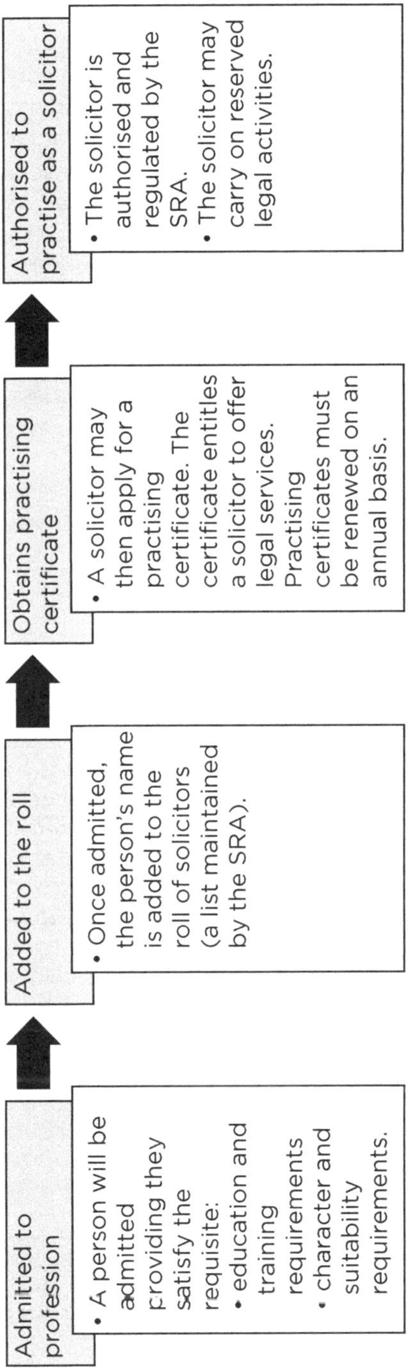

Figure 5.2: Authorisation requirements for solicitors

practice *only* conducts activities that are *not* reserved legal activities, *or* they provide any reserved legal activities through an authorised body. Such solicitors must also meet the additional conditions set out in regulation 10 of the Authorisation of Individuals Regulations. Sometimes solicitors are employed by a company or organisation to provide that employer with legal advice and assistance. These solicitors are known as 'in-house' solicitors. They may carry on reserved legal activities for their employer, but they cannot offer such services to the general public. Additionally, solicitors working within non-commercial organisations (such as charities, not-for-profit organisations, independent trade unions and community interest groups) may, on behalf of the organisation, provide reserved legal activities to the public. All other solicitors carrying on reserved legal activities must have a valid practising certificate and must provide reserved activities through an authorised firm.

Authorisation of firms

As noted above, reserved legal activities must usually be provided through an authorised firm. **Table 5.3** outlines the types of bodies that may be authorised by the SRA to provide legal services (see also **Practice example 5.2**).

Table 5.3: Types of bodies that may be authorised to provide legal services

Recognised bodies	A firm will be eligible to apply for SRA authorisation as a *recognised* body if they are deemed to be a 'legal services body' (under s 9A of the Administration of Justice Act 1985) and all of the managers and interest holders are legally qualified. Recognised bodies take different forms. Many solicitors' firms operate as *partnerships*. Such firms are owned and run by partners, who employ solicitors and administration staff to work for them. Some firms are *limited liability partnerships* (LLP). LLPs have members, rather than partners. Some law practices are *companies* registered under the Companies Act 2006.
Licensed bodies	Non-lawyers may own and manage law practices. Such practices are known as alternative business structures (ABSs) and may apply for authorisation as a *licensed* body. A licensed body must have at least one manager who is authorised by the SRA or another approved regulator.
Recognised sole practice	Some solicitors work on an individual basis in a practice providing reserved legal activities to the public. Such organisations must be authorised by the SRA as a *recognised sole practice*.

Practice example 5.2

Two friends decide to set up a company that deals exclusively with will writing. They plan on offering will-writing services to members of the public. Neither of the friends are solicitors. Do the friends need to apply for SRA authorisation for the proposed company?

No. Will writing is not a reserved legal activity. The friends are not solicitors and do not, therefore, require their company to be authorised by the SRA.

Principles

The SRA Standards and Regulations are underpinned by seven core principles. The SRA Principles outline the fundamental principles of ethical behaviour that solicitors are expected to adhere to. They apply to any individual authorised by the SRA to provide legal services. The principles require that solicitors act:

1) in a way that upholds the constitutional principle of the rule of law, and the proper administration of justice
2) in a way that upholds public trust and confidence in the solicitors' profession and in legal services provided by authorised persons
3) with independence
4) with honesty
5) with integrity
6) in a way that encourages equality, diversity and inclusion
7) in the best interests of each client.

The aim of the principles is to ensure that solicitors fulfil their responsibilities to their clients and to the public at large. As you can see, the first two principles concern the proper administration of justice and preserving confidence in the profession. The remaining principles are concerned with obligations owed to clients. Collectively, they require solicitors to adopt high standards of integrity and professionalism. For the SQE, you will need to familiarise yourself with these principles.

To ensure that firms and solicitors operate at a professional level, the SRA has laid out specific duties, rules and guidelines in its Standards and Regulations. All solicitors and authorised firms are expected to adhere to the applicable regulations and codes of conduct. The SRA is responsible for enforcing compliance with its Standards and Regulations.

Revision tip

It is important to note that ethics and professional conduct are examined pervasively across both of the SQE1 assessments and the SQE2 assessments. It is, therefore, vital that you understand the various ethical and professional duties that apply to solicitors and can identify when a question or task involves an ethical or professional conduct issue. These topics are covered in detail in ***Revise SQE: Ethics and Professional Conduct***.

Risk-based regulation

Section 1 of the LSA outlines the regulatory objectives that each regulatory body must try to achieve. The regulatory objectives are:

(a) protecting and promoting the public interest
(b) supporting the constitutional principle of the rule of law
(c) improving access to justice
(d) protecting and promoting the interests of consumers
(e) promoting competition in the provision of services
(f) encouraging an independent, strong, diverse and effective legal profession
(g) increasing public understanding of the citizen's legal rights and duties
(h) promoting and maintaining adherence to the professional principles
(i) promoting the prevention and detection of economic crime.

The SRA adopts **a risk-based approach to regulation**.

Key term: risk-based regulation

The risk-based regulation model assesses risk according to the likely impact of a risk materialising and the probability of the risk materialising. This model of regulation is commonly adopted by regulators.

Applying this approach, the SRA identifies risks that might adversely impact its ability to meet any of the regulatory objectives. The SRA then compares and ranks different risks. This enables it to determine which risks to prioritise and allocate its resources to. The risk-based model of regulation is common in industries and professions where the regulator has finite resources. It is not feasible for the SRA to detect and enforce every possible breach of its rules. The risk-based model allows the SRA to target its resources at the risk it considers to be most significant.

In this context, risk is evaluated by reference to *impact* and *probability*. Impact refers to what is at risk and probability refers to how likely it is that an event will occur. Risk is therefore evaluated according to the probable *impact* of the risk materialising *and* the *probability* (likelihood) of the risk materialising. Where an identified risk is likely to cause a significant impact (eg it is likely to affect many firms and/or clients) and is very likely to materialise (eg indicators suggest there is a high chance of the event occurring), the risk is likely to be considered a priority and resources are likely to be allocated to addressing it. A risk may relate to a specific solicitor or firm or it may relate to the profession as a whole. The SRA's response to an identified risk should be proportionate to the risk that has been identified. For example, if the SRA has received complaints about a specific solicitor within a firm, it may decide to place restrictions on the type of work the solicitor is permitted to undertake. If it believes there is risk concerning the profession as a whole, it may choose to amend its regulations or codes of conduct. The SRA also requires firms to identify, monitor and manage risks through compliance with risk assessment regulations.

The SRA regularly publishes information and guidance concerning risks on its website. For instance, it publishes 'Risk Outlook reports', thematic reviews and 'warning notices' which highlight specific regulatory risks. By way of example, the SRA has recently published a report and a warning notice concerning inadequate money laundering controls.

Key term: warning notices

A warning notice is a formal communication from the SRA that alerts solicitors to serious regulatory risks or misconduct trends, and provides guidance on expected standards of behaviour and compliance requirements. They are designed to prevent misconduct and help solicitors understand how to comply with relevant professional standards.

Revision tip

Remember that ethics and professional conduct is examined pervasively across the two SQE1 assessments and can be examined across *all* subject areas. As with the other subject areas assessed in SQE1, questions will be based on realistic client-based problems and situations *which can include those set out in relevant SRA warning notices.* Given this explicit reference to warning notices, you are strongly advised to read all of the warning notices published on the SRA website in preparation for the SQE1 assessments. This will help you to identify questions that involve regulatory risks and/or professional conduct issues and will help you to understand what the SRA expects or requires solicitors to do to mitigate such risks and ensure compliance with professional standards.

Professional indemnity insurance

Occasionally, the standard of service provided by a solicitor falls below an acceptable level and causes a client to suffer some form of loss or damage. In such circumstances, a client may bring a civil claim against the solicitor. If the claim is successful, the client may be entitled to receive a sum of money to compensate them for the loss suffered. Such claims can be costly to defend and can result in a firm/solicitor being liable to pay significant sums of money. **Professional indemnity insurance** (PII) is designed to cover the payment of such liabilities. Generally, it also covers the costs associated with defending such claims. Having such cover in place helps to maintain confidence in the profession. For this reason, all SRA authorised firms and freelance solicitors are required to have appropriate PII in place.

Key term: professional indemnity insurance (PII)

In this context, PII provides cover to the insured party (the law firm or solicitor) should they breach a professional duty that causes financial loss or damage to a client.

The relevant requirements are outlined in the SRA Indemnity Insurance Rules. The key requirements to note are as follows:

- *All* authorised bodies must acquire and maintain appropriate PII. The insurance policy must provide cover in accordance with the minimum terms and conditions (MTCs) stipulated by the SRA. The PII policy must provide *adequate* and *appropriate* cover for the services the firm provides. In some cases, the level of coverage will necessarily exceed the MTCs.
- Each firm/solicitor must determine what level of coverage is appropriate to their specific circumstances. What is considered adequate and appropriate for a firm/a solicitor is likely to change over time. When determining what is adequate and appropriate, firms and solicitors should consider factors such as:
  - the nature of work undertaken
  - the number and type of clients
  - the possible value of any claim liabilities
  - any history of claims against the firm/solicitor
  - alternative arrangements to meet liabilities.
- Recognised and licensed bodies must be insured for at least £3 million for any one claim (exclusive of defence costs). In all other cases the sum insured for must be at least £2 million.
- Where a solicitor works on a freelance basis and carries out reserved legal activities, they are obliged to take out and maintain appropriate

PII. Solicitors working in non-commercial bodies that are providing reserved legal services to the public must ensure that the body takes out insurance that meets the 'adequate and appropriate' requirement.
- The PII policy must be renewed on an annual basis. Insurance coverage must be continuous (ie the new policy must come into effect when the existing policy comes to an end).
- Solicitors/firms must be transparent and honest about their PII provision.

Revision tip

Remember that compliance with the MTCs will not always discharge the obligation to have adequate and appropriate PII. As the name suggests, the *minimum* terms and conditions are the 'baseline' of what must be covered in the PII policy (see **Practice example 5.3**).

The SRA website provides guidance on professional indemnity insurance requirements. You are advised to read the guidance in full and check it regularly to ensure you are aware of any updates.

Practice example 5.3

A small law firm that ordinarily deals with low value personal injury claims takes on a complex clinical negligence case. The estimated value of the claim is in excess of £4 million. The firm have PII cover of £3 million.

Would this level of PII coverage likely satisfy the SRA's requirement to have adequate and appropriate indemnity insurance?

A claim of this value and type could expose the firm to a claim for the full value of the medical negligence claim *plus* costs. Medical negligence claims are subject to strict time limits and the case is described as complex; both these factors increase the probability of negligence occurring. The size and type of the firm means it is unlikely to have the resources to meet any substantial costs itself. In these circumstances, cover of £3 million is unlikely to be considered appropriate.

■ KEY POINT CHECKLIST

- The statutory framework for the regulation of legal services is laid out in the Legal Services Act 2007. The LSA classifies certain legal activities as 'reserved'. Reserved legal activities may only be carried on by authorised legal professionals. Authorised persons are subject to regulation by the relevant regulatory body.

- Reserved legal activities are listed in s 12 of the Act and include: the exercise of a right of audience, the conduct of litigation, reserved instrument activities, probate activities, notarial activities and the administration of oaths.
- The SRA is the independent regulatory body of the Law Society of England and Wales.
- Once admitted and added to the roll, a solicitor may apply for a practising certificate, which entitles a solicitor to carry on all reserved legal activities (except notarial activities). Solicitors holding a practising certificate are authorised to carry on reserved legal activities, but these must usually be provided through an authorised firm/body.
- The SRA can authorise recognised sole practices, recognised bodies and licensed bodies.
- *All* solicitors and authorised firms must abide by the same professional principles and codes of conduct. These principles and codes of conduct are set by the SRA and are contained within the SRA Standards and Regulations.
- The SRA Standards and Regulations are underpinned by seven core principles. The aim of the SRA Principles is to ensure that solicitors fulfil their responsibilities to their clients and to the public at large.
- The SRA adopts a risk-based model of regulation. Risk is evaluated according to impact and probability.
- The SRA also publishes information and guidance on regulatory risks on its website. These resources (eg thematic reports, warning notices, Risk Outlook reports etc) are designed to bring specific risks to the attention of solicitors so that they are aware of regulatory and non-compliance issues/trends, and understand what the SRA expects in terms of compliance and behaviour.
- The SRA Indemnity Insurance Rules require all authorised firms to take out *and* maintain PII.
- PII cover must meet the minimum requirements and provide 'adequate' and 'appropriate' cover.

■ KEY TERMS AND CONCEPTS

- reserved legal activities (**page 89**)
- risk-based regulation (**page 98**)
- warning notice (**page 99**)
- professional indemnity insurance (PII) (**page 100**)

SQE1-STYLE QUESTIONS

QUESTION 1

A solicitor is authorised to provide legal services by the SRA. The solicitor has a valid practising certificate.

Which of the following best describes the effect of authorisation?

A. The solicitor may carry on all reserved legal activities.

B. The solicitor may carry on all reserved legal activities and must adhere to regulation by the SRA in respect of any reserved legal activities they carry on.

C. The solicitor may carry on all reserved legal activities and must adhere to the relevant statutory regulations.

D. The solicitor may carry on all reserved legal activities, except notarial activities, and must adhere to regulation by the SRA in respect of all legal services they provide.

E. The solicitor may carry on all reserved legal activities, except notarial activities, and is subject to regulation by the SRA in respect of such activities.

QUESTION 2

An authorised firm specialises in high-value commercial contract work. They have a number of large offices across the north-west of England. The firm has PII cover of £3 million.

Would this level of PII coverage likely satisfy the SRA's requirement to have adequate and appropriate indemnity insurance?

A. The PII coverage complies with the SRA MTCs so would meet with adequate and appropriate requirement.

B. The PII coverage meets the requirements stipulated in the SRA Indemnity Insurance Rules so would meet with adequate and appropriate requirement.

C. The PII coverage may not be considered to be adequate and appropriate because of the size of the firm and the nature of the work it undertakes.

D. The PII coverage may not be considered to be adequate and appropriate because it has not complied with the minimum level of coverage stipulated in the MTCs.

E. The PII coverage may not be considered to be adequate and appropriate because it has not complied with the minimum level of coverage stipulated in the SRA Indemnity Insurance Rules.

QUESTION 3

A woman successfully applies for a job in a law firm. The role is for the position of a civil litigation solicitor. The law firm is authorised by the SRA. The woman used to work as a solicitor. For the last three years, she has worked as a university lecturer. During this period, she did not renew her practising certificate.

Which of the following statements most accurately describes her position?

A. The woman is appropriately qualified and is entitled to offer legal services through an authorised body. She does not need to apply for a practising certificate to take up the job offer.
B. If the woman accepted the role without obtaining a practising certificate, she would only be able to offer non-reserved legal services.
C. If the woman accepted the role without obtaining a practising certificate, she may commit a criminal offence should she carry on any reserved legal activities.
D. The woman is a qualified solicitor and is therefore entitled to take up the job offer. She may apply for a practising certificate if she wants to carry on any reserved legal activities.
E. The woman must obtain a practising certificate to take up the job offer. The role is that of a solicitor so she must have a valid practising certificate. Acting as a solicitor without a valid practising certificate is a criminal offence.

QUESTION 4

A solicitor is considering practising on a freelance basis.

Which of the following statements most accurately describes the relevant authorisation requirements the solicitor must comply with should they decide to operate on a freelance basis?

A. The solicitor must obtain SRA authorisation and operate as a sole registered practice if they intend to carry on reserved legal activities.

B. The solicitor must obtain SRA authorisation to operate as a sole registered practice.
C. The solicitor must provide any reserved legal services through an approved firm/body.
D. The solicitor is required to operate as a sole registered practice.
E. The solicitor must obtain SRA authorisation to operate as a sole registered practice regardless of whether they intend to carry on reserved legal activities.

QUESTION 5

A chartered legal executive works for a law firm authorised by the SRA. They engage in reserved legal activities.

Which of the following statements most accurately describes the relevant regulatory requirements?

A. The legal executive is subject to regulation by CILEx Regulation. The firm they work in is subject to regulation by the SRA.
B. The legal executive is regulated by the SRA because they work for an authorised firm. The firm is also regulated by the SRA.
C. The legal executive is regulated by the SRA because they carry on reserved legal activities. The firm is regulated by the SRA.
D. The legal executive is subject to regulation by the Legal Service Board. The firm is regulated by CILEx Regulation.
E. The legal executive and the firm are subject to regulation by CILEx Regulation.

■ ANSWERS TO QUESTIONS

Answers to 'What do you know already?' questions at the start of the chapter

1) The answer is 'false'. The SRA regulate solicitors (including registered European lawyers and registered foreign lawyers) and law firms. Other legal service providers are regulated by separate approved regulatory bodies (outlined in **Table 5.2**).
2) The following activities are classified as 'reserved legal activities' under s 12 LSA 2007:
   - issuing a civil claim in the County Court
   - appearing in the Crown Court on behalf of a client

- drafting probate papers
- administering an oath.

3) PII is designed to ensure that when professional negligence occurs there is adequate provision to meet any claims that might be brought against a firm or solicitor.
4) The seven principles set out in the SRA Standards and Regulations require solicitors to act:
   1. in a way that upholds the constitutional principle of the rule of law, and the proper administration of justice
   2. in a way that upholds public trust and confidence in the solicitors' profession and in legal services provided by authorised persons
   3. with independence
   4. with honesty
   5. with integrity
   6. in a way that encourages equality, diversity and inclusion
   7. in the best interests of each client.
5) Risk-based regulation assesses risk according to the likely impact of a risk materialising and the probability of the risk materialising. This model of regulation is commonly adopted by regulators. It allows the regulator to target finite resources at areas it considers to pose the greatest risk.

Answers to end-of-chapter SQE1-style questions

Question 1:

The correct answer was D. All solicitors are subject to regulation by the SRA. Authorisation does not allow a solicitor to engage in *all* reserved legal activities because they cannot carry on notarial activities. Options A, B and C are therefore incorrect. Option E is incorrect because regulation by the SRA applies to all legal activities, not just reserved activities.

Question 2:

The correct answer was C. Whether PII coverage is considered adequate and appropriate depends on whether it is suitable for the specific firm, taking into account the firm's specific circumstances. Options B and E are incorrect because the minimum level of coverage is stipulated in the MTCs. Options A and D are incorrect because compliance with the MTCs does not determine whether the level of coverage is adequate and appropriate.

Question 3:

The correct answer was E. It is a criminal offence to act as a solicitor without a practising certificate. A practising certificate is a requirement irrespective of whether the solicitor plans to carry on reserved legal activities. Options A, B, C and D are therefore incorrect.

Question 4:

The correct answer was C. Freelance solicitors may provide reserved legal activities through an approved firm/body. Freelance solicitors are only required to register as sole registered practices if they want to offer reserved legal services through their practice. Options A, B, D and E are incorrect as they all suggest that registration as a sole registered practice is a requirement for all freelance solicitors.

Question 5:

The correct answer was A. Chartered legal executives are subject to the regulation of their approved regulatory body, CILEx Regulation (therefore options B and C are wrong). The firm is authorised by the SRA and is therefore regulated by the SRA (therefore options D and E are wrong).

■ KEY CASES, RULES, STATUTES AND INSTRUMENTS

The SQE1 Assessment Specification does not require you to know any case names, or statutory materials, for this topic. You are, however, strongly encouraged to familiarise yourself with the key provisions of the Legal Services Act 2007 and the SRA Standards and Regulations. You are also advised to regularly check the SRA website for further information and guidance concerning regulatory risks (eg warning notices).

6

Overriding legal obligations

MAKE SURE YOU KNOW

This chapter deals with the overriding legal obligations that all legal professionals, regulated or otherwise, must comply with. For the SQE, you need to understand the overriding legal obligations that stem from the Equality Act 2010 and anti-money laundering legislation. While such obligations apply to other service providers, this chapter focuses on the obligations that apply to solicitors and law firms.

It is important to highlight that in any SQE1 sitting (FLK1 and FLK2), Ethics and Professional Conduct and money laundering questions can make up to 20% of the questions assessed (money laundering questions being assessed in FLK1 only). It is, therefore, vital that you have a good knowledge and understanding of anti-money laundering regulations and legislation.

- **The Equality Act 2010**
  - Key concepts:
    - protected characteristics
    - prohibited conduct
  - Solicitors' obligations as 'service providers'
  - Solicitors' obligations as 'employers'
- **Anti-money laundering legislation**
  - Purpose of anti-money laundering legislation
  - Money laundering regulations (including due diligence measures)
  - Circumstances where knowledge or suspicions of money laundering must be reported
  - The appropriate:
    - person/body to receive such reports
    - time for such reports to be made
    - procedure for making such reports
  - Offences and defences under POCA

■ SQE ASSESSMENT ADVICE

As you work through this chapter, remember to pay particular attention in your revision to:

- the legal obligations that stem from the Equality Act 2010
- the purpose of anti-money laundering legislation
- the circumstances where suspicion of money laundering should be reported
- the appropriate person or body to whom suspicions should be reported
- the appropriate time for such reports to be made and the appropriate procedure to be followed
- direct involvement and non-direct involvement offences, and defences to those offences under the Proceeds of Crime Act 2002 (POCA)
- due diligence requirements.

The SQE1 Assessment Specification has identified that you must know the following statutes:

- Equality Act 2010
- Proceeds of Crime Act 2002.

■ WHAT DO YOU KNOW ALREADY?

Have a go at these questions before reading this chapter. If you find some difficult or cannot remember the answers, make a note to look more closely at that during your revision.

1) Explain the key difference between direct discrimination and indirect discrimination.

   [The Equality Act 2010, page 110]

2) List the non-direct involvement offences under POCA.

   [The Proceeds of Crime Act 2002, page 124]

3) True or false: solicitors are not under a legal duty to report *suspicions* of money laundering to the relevant nominated officer. They are, however, legally obliged to report *knowledge* of money laundering to the relevant nominated officer.

   [Reporting requirements, page 122]

4) Which of the following defences are applicable to direct-involvement offences under POCA?

   a) Reasonable excuse defence

   b) Overseas defence

   c) Training defence

   d) Legal professional privilege defence.

   [Defences to money laundering offences, page 128]

5) What is customer due diligence?

   [Due diligence requirements, page 120]

THE EQUALITY ACT 2010

The overarching ethos of the Equality Act 2010 ('the Act') is that everyone is entitled to be treated fairly. The Act aims to eliminate unjustifiable discrimination and unfair treatment. Solicitors have legal obligations under the Act because they provide legal services. Some solicitors have additional legal obligations under the Act because they are employers. These overriding legal obligations are distinct from other duties imposed on solicitors by the Solicitors Regulation Authority (SRA).

Key concepts: protected characteristics

The Act identifies a number of personal characteristics that are the subject of protection under the legislation. These are known as **protected characteristics**. Section 4 specifies the nine protected characteristics, which are outlined in **Table 6.1**.

Key term: protected characteristics

Protected characteristics are the personal characteristics that are safeguarded by virtue of the Equality Act 2010.

Table 6.1: Protected characteristics

Protected characteristic	Explanation
Age	Protects a person being subject to unfair treatment because they belong to a particular age group.
Disability	A person has the protected characteristic of disability if they have a physical or mental impairment *and* the impairment has a substantial and long-term adverse effect on their ability to carry out normal day-to-day activities.
Gender reassignment	A person has the protected characteristic of gender reassignment if the person is proposing to undergo, is undergoing or has undergone a process (or part of a process) for the purpose of reassigning the person's sex by changing physiological or other attributes.
Marriage/civil partnerships	A person has the protected characteristic of marriage or civil partnership if they are married or in a civil partnership.

Table 6.1: Continued

Protected characteristic	Explanation
Pregnancy and maternity	Pregnancy/maternity is one of the protected characteristics listed in s 4.
Race	Protects a person from being treated unfairly because of their race or racial group. Race includes colour, nationality or ethnic or national origins.
Religion or beliefs	Protects a person from being subjected to unfair treatment because of their religious or philosophical beliefs or absence of such beliefs.
Sex	Protects a person from being subject to unfair treatment because of their sex.
Sexual orientation	Sexual orientation means a person's sexual orientation towards • persons of the same sex • persons of the opposite sex, or • persons of the same sex and the opposite sex.

Exam warning

In the SQE, it is likely that you will be tested on your ability to accurately identify whether a realistic client-based scenario involves one of the nine protected characteristics. Make sure that you can recall each of the characteristics.

It is also possible that you will be required to determine whether actions described in a realistic client-based problem or situation constitute prohibited conduct under the Act and why this is so. It is, therefore, important that you have a good knowledge and understanding of the different forms of prohibited conduct under the legislation (outlined in the sections below).

Key concepts: prohibited conduct

The Act defines certain types of discriminatory behaviour, known as **prohibited conduct**.

Key term: prohibited conduct

In this context, prohibited conduct refers to behaviour that is unlawful under the Equality Act 2010.

The following section provides a brief overview of the key types of prohibited conduct.

Direct discrimination

Put simply, direct discrimination occurs where a person is treated less favourably than someone else would have been in the same situation *and* that difference in treatment is because of one of the protected characteristics. For example, a person's application for a job is overlooked *because* of their ethnic origin. The key components of direct discrimination are illustrated in **Figure 6.1**.

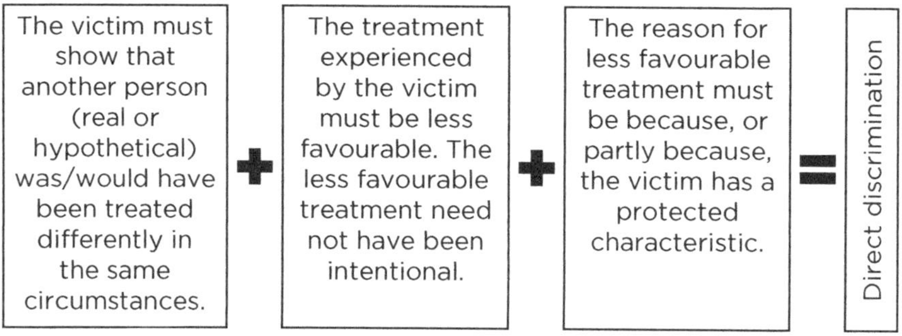

Figure 6.1: Direct discrimination

Indirect discrimination

Indirect discrimination is more subtle than direct discrimination. It occurs when a policy, practice or rule applies generally but has the effect of adversely impacting those who share a protected characteristic. For example, indirect discrimination might occur because an employer applies a policy that requires employees to travel at very short notice. While the policy applies to all employees, it is likely to adversely impact female employees because they are more likely to have childcare responsibilities that make travelling at short notice challenging. Indirect discrimination may be justified where the policy, rule or practice aims to achieve a legitimate aim. In the example above, the employer would need to show that the policy has a legitimate aim. To be justified, the discrimination must be a *proportionate* way of achieving the legitimate aim.

Discrimination arising from disability

Disability discrimination occurs where a person treats a disabled person unfavourably because of the person's disability *or* because of something arising from the disability. A claimant is not required to compare the treatment they received with the treatment of others with a disability (as is required in direct discrimination cases). Again, it may be possible to justify less favourable treatment if it can be demonstrated to be a proportionate means of achieving a legitimate aim.

Harassment

Harassment occurs when a person is subjected to unwanted conduct that relates to certain protected characteristics (age, disability, gender reassignment, race, religion or belief, sex or sexual orientation) *and* the unwanted conduct violates the victim's dignity, or creates an intimidating, hostile, degrading, humiliating or offensive environment for that person. Harassment also occurs where the unwanted conduct is of a sexual nature and has the effect of violating the victim's dignity or creating an intimidating, hostile, degrading, humiliating or offensive environment for the victim, and the victim is treated less favourably than they would have been treated because they rejected or submitted to the unwanted conduct.

Test whether you can identify whether harassment has occurred in **Practice example 6.1**.

Practice example 6.1

A senior solicitor in a firm makes unwanted sexual advances towards a trainee solicitor. Those advances are rejected. As a result of this, the solicitor allocates the trainee solicitor tedious administrative tasks, refuses to acknowledge the trainee solicitor in the communal areas of the building and tells other members of staff in the firm that the trainee is 'frigid'.

Would such behaviour amount to harassment under the Act?

It is likely that this behaviour would amount to harassment. The conduct is of a sexual nature and has created an intimidating and hostile working environment. The rejection of the conduct is likely to have caused the victim to be treated less favourably than they would have been had they not rejected the behaviour.

Victimisation

Victimisation occurs where a person subjects another person to a detriment (a disadvantage) because they believe that person has done, or will do, a protected act. A protected act includes:

- bringing proceedings under the Equality Act
- giving evidence or information in proceedings brought under the Equality Act

- doing anything that is related to the provisions of the Equality Act
- alleging that another person has done something in breach of the Equality Act.

Revision tip

It is important to note that a victim of victimisation does not need to establish that they have a protected characteristic.

Try to answer **Practice example 6.2** to test your ability to identify prohibited conduct.

Practice example 6.2

A firm of solicitors advertises an internal vacancy. It receives several applications. A senior solicitor rejects one of the applications because it is from a man who experiences severe depression. The solicitor tells his personal assistant that 'people with depression are a nightmare to manage'. The personal assistant is appalled by this comment and reports it to the firm's partners. The assistant indicates that she will support the man in a claim against the firm unless the behaviour is addressed. She is told that if she does this, she will lose the opportunity to be promoted.

Which, if any, of the above behaviour amounts to prohibited conduct under the Act?

The actions of the senior solicitor amount to direct discrimination and disability discrimination. The man with depression has been treated unfavourably compared to the other applicants and the treatment is a consequence of him having a disability. The treatment of the assistant would amount to victimisation. She has been deprived of the chance of promotion because the firm believed she may do a protected act (eg giving evidence against the firm).

Duty to make adjustments

The Act also imposes certain *positive* duties. This includes a duty to make reasonable adjustments for disabled persons (s 20). A failure to comply with this duty amounts to discrimination under s 21. Reasonable steps must be taken to prevent a disabled person being put at a *substantial* disadvantage because of:

- a provision, criterion or practice (eg the practice of only providing information in a standard format)
- a physical feature (eg not having wheelchair access)
- lack of provision of an auxiliary aid.

Solicitors' obligations as service providers

The anti-discriminatory provisions of the Act, outlined above, apply to those providing services to members of the public. Therefore, they apply to solicitors and other legal services providers. Under s 29, service providers are prohibited from treating service users in certain ways. For our purposes, the service provider is a solicitor providing legal services (including free services). The service user would be a client or prospective client.

A solicitor must not:

- discriminate against or victimise a client or prospective client in respect of terms of service
- discriminate against or victimise a client by terminating services provided to a client/prospective client
- discriminate against or victimise a client by subjecting the client to any other detriment
- harass a client/prospective client.

Now take a look at **Practice example 6.3** to see how your knowledge of this topic might be tested in a client-based scenario.

Practice example 6.3

A solicitor discovers one of her clients is bisexual and, as a result of this, refuses to continue to provide pro bono services to the client. Is the solicitor's behaviour lawful?

This is a clear example of a solicitor discriminating against a client with a protected characteristic (sexual orientation) in a way prohibited by s 29.

Making adjustments

A solicitor will be deemed to have discriminated against a disabled person if they fail to comply with the duty to make *reasonable* adjustments as outlined above. The duty is owed to 'disabled people generally' and is anticipatory in nature. In essence, this means that firms must adopt a proactive rather than reactive approach. For example, a firm of solicitors should take reasonable steps to ensure that a disabled person can access their building (eg make provision for wheelchair access), regardless of whether a disabled client has raised an issue regarding such access. The cost of making reasonable adjustments cannot be passed on to the client. When assessing whether it is reasonable to expect a solicitor or firm to make adjustments, a court will consider factors such as the cost of making the adjustment and the resources of the firm.

Solicitors' obligations as employers

Sections 39 and 40 deal with the obligations that solicitors owe to their employees and to prospective employees.

Unlawful acts: prospective employees

It is unlawful to harass a prospective employee. It is also unlawful for an employer to subject a prospective employee to discrimination or victimisation in respect of:

- recruitment arrangements
- declining to offer employment
- terms of employment.

For example, a firm could not discriminate against an applicant by refusing to accept applications from people of a particular age group (eg people aged over 40) for no objectively justifiable reason.

Unlawful acts: employees

Employees in law firms are protected under the Act. Employers must not subject an employee to harassment and must not discriminate against or victimise an employee:

- as to the terms of employment
- in the way it affords access to opportunities for promotion, transfer or training, or for receiving any other benefit, facility or service
- by dismissing the employee, or
- by subjecting the employee to any detriment.

Making adjustments: employees and prospective employees

Employers must also make reasonable adjustments for disabled employees and prospective employees. Failure to comply with this duty will amount to discrimination. It is important to note that employers are *only* required to make such adjustments where they *know, or ought to know*, that an employee is disabled *and* is likely to suffer a disadvantage. For example, a firm is not obliged to modify workstations in case they hire a disabled employee. The duty to make such an adjustment would arise when a disabled person was recruited to the firm.

Take a look at **Practice Example 6.4** and try to identify whether the firm has made a reasonable adjustment.

Practice example 6.4

A woman with Asperger's syndrome applies for a job as a trainee solicitor. As part of the recruitment process, all applicants are required to undertake and pass an online multiple-choice test. She requests to be able to have the format of her test altered because, as a result of her condition, she would be disadvantaged by the multiple-choice question (MCQ) format of the test. Her request is refused.

Has the employer breached their duty to make an adjustment for this applicant?

These facts are based on the case facts of the *Government Legal Service v Brookes* UKEAT 0302/16. The Government Legal Service was deemed to have failed to make reasonable adjustments for the claimant. The woman was deemed to have been subjected to indirect discrimination and disability discrimination.

Vicarious liability

An employer may be held vicariously liable for the unlawful acts of their employees committed in the course of employment. The employer may be liable even where they were unaware of or condemned the employee's conduct. Employees remain liable for their behaviour. Employers may escape liability if they can show that they took reasonable steps to prevent such behaviour (eg by providing appropriate training).

Positive action

Firms may want to take positive steps to address an apparent equality issue. The Act permits, in limited situations, positive discrimination. This means that in some circumstances an employer may treat an employee or prospective employee more favourably because they have a protected characteristic. Positive action is only lawful where the firm reasonably believes that persons who share a protected characteristic:

- suffer a disadvantage connected to the characteristic, or
- have different needs, or
- are disproportionately underrepresented in respect of a particular activity, and
- the positive action taken by the firm is a proportionate way of redressing the situation.

For example, a firm may feel that staff who share a protected characteristic have additional needs that require additional resources. Section 159 also permits positive action in respect of recruitment and promotion. Where an employer reasonably thinks that persons with a particular protected characteristic are disadvantaged or disproportionately underrepresented, they may treat a person with the protected characteristic more favourably than others who do not share that protected characteristic.

Revision tip

It is important to note that positive action is *only* permitted where the candidate with the protected characteristic is as suitable for the role as other candidates. Positive action could only be used where there is a tiebreak situation between equally suitable candidates.

MONEY LAUNDERING

Money laundering is used by criminals to try to conceal the unlawful source of money (or property) acquired as a result of criminal activity, as illustrated in **Figure 6.2**.

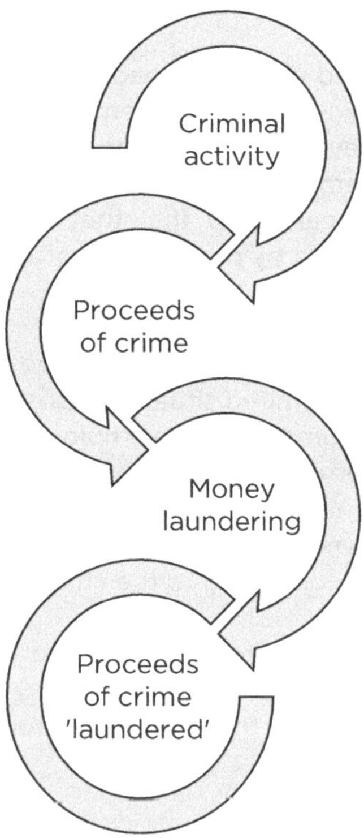

Figure 6.2: Money laundering

Key term: money laundering

Money laundering is a method used by criminals to make it appear as though **proceeds of crime** derive from a legitimate source.

Key term: proceeds of crime

The term 'proceeds of crime' refers to the benefits that flow from criminal activity. For example, property that has been stolen or fraudulently obtained are proceeds of crime. Money generated from conducting criminal activity (eg selling drugs) are proceeds of crime.

Money laundering involves the three stages shown in **Figure 6.3**.

Placement	→	Layering	→	Integration
Money from criminal activity is introduced into the financial system.		The money passes through a number of parties or transactions to distance it from the criminal activity.		The money is integrated back into the financial system and the criminal takes possession of the 'laundered' money.

Figure 6.3: Money laundering stages

Revision tip

You may find it useful to think of money laundering as a process whereby 'dirty' money derived from criminal activity is 'washed' so that it becomes 'clean' money that appears to originate from a legitimate source.

Purpose and scope of anti-money laundering legislation

Money laundering is directly connected to serious crime. Because solicitors handle money and deal with transactions on behalf of clients, criminals sometimes try to use solicitors to launder money. Laundering can be complex and may involve many transactions or parties or may involve money moving between different countries. Such arrangements make it very difficult to trace the funds to the original source and prosecute those involved in serious crime. A global response to money laundering is therefore necessary. The Financial Action Task Force is the global money laundering and terrorist financing watchdog. It is an inter-governmental body that sets international standards designed to prevent money laundering. It recommends that countries implement domestic laws to meet these international standards. In the UK, the relevant law is contained in the Money Laundering, Terrorist Financing and Transfer of Funds (Information on the Payer) Regulations 2017 (SI 2017/692) (MLRs) and POCA. The MLRs impose numerous duties on law firms. **Table 6.2** summarises the key duties that derive from the MLRs.

Table 6.2: Key duties under MLRs

Regulation	Overview of duty
Regulation 18	Firms must maintain a written risk assessment that identifies and assesses the risk of the firm being used for money laundering.
Regulation 19	Firms must establish and maintain *policies, controls and procedures* to mitigate and manage the money laundering risks identified in the risk assessment.
Regulation 21	Firms must appoint a *money laundering compliance officer (MLCO)* to be responsible for the firm's compliance with the MLRs. The firm must also appoint a *nominated officer*, often referred to as the *money laundering reporting officer (MLRO)*. The nominated officer receives internal reports of suspicious activity and, where appropriate, must make Suspicious Activity Reports (SARs) to the National Crime Agency (NCA). The SRA must be notified of any changes to the identity of the MLCO or MLRO.
Regulation 24	Firms must provide staff with appropriate training on money laundering and maintain records of the training staff have undertaken.
Regulations 27 and 28	Firms must verify the identity of each of their clients. This is known as **customer due diligence** (CDD). The verification *must* take place as soon as possible after first contact. Records of CDD documents and supporting evidence must be retained for five years.

Revision tip

Remember that the SRA publishes detailed guidance to help solicitors understand their obligations under anti-money laundering regulations and legislation. You are advised to read this guidance, which is published on the SRA website, in full.

Due diligence requirements

As noted in **Table 6.2**, solicitors must comply with **CDD measures**. CDD is a process of checks solicitors use to identify a client and make sure they are who they say they are.

Key term: customer due diligence (CDD)

In this context, CDD refers to the measures in place to identify and verify a client so as to reduce the risk of money laundering.

Solicitors must carry out CDD when:

- forming a business relationship
- carrying out an occasional transaction that amounts to or exceeds €15,000 (approximately £12,600)
- the solicitor suspects money laundering
- the solicitor doubts the accuracy or adequacy of documents or information previously provided for CDD purposes.

A solicitor must verify a client's identity based on a reliable independent source (such as a passport or other official photographic ID and proof of address). CDD must take place as soon as is practicable. In cases where the client is not an individual person (eg the client is a company, trust or similar), the solicitor must take steps to verify the identity of any beneficial owner and take measures to understand the ownership and control of the business structure.

Corporate bodies

Where a client is a corporate body, solicitors must obtain and verify:

- its name
- its company number (or other registration)
- the address of its registered office and, if different, its principal place of business
- where the corporate body is not listed on a regulated market, the solicitor should ascertain the law the body is subject to, its constitution (or other governing documents) and the names of the board of directors (or equivalent management body) and the senior persons responsible for its operations.

Simplified due diligence

Simplified due diligence is permitted where the business relationship or transaction presents a low risk of money laundering. For example, where the company is a well-known financial institution or company whose securities (eg shares) are listed on a regulated market. In such circumstances, a solicitor is permitted to adopt simplified due diligence (eg simply obtain confirmation of the company's listing on the Stock Exchange).

Enhanced due diligence

Enhanced due diligence (EDD), as the name suggests, is a more thorough verification process and is used where the risk of money laundering is higher than usual. As a minimum, EDD must involve:

- examining the background and purpose of the transaction
- increased monitoring of the business relationship.

Typically, EDD involves taking *additional* steps to verify a client's identity and understand the background, ownership and financial situation of the customer, and other parties to the transaction. This usually involves obtaining additional information for reliable sources.

EDD must be applied where the transaction or business relationship involves the following:

- A person established in a high-risk third country (eg one that has a deficient anti-money laundering regime).
- A politically exposed person (PEP). A PEP is someone who has been appointed by a community institution, an international body or a state, to a high-profile position within the last 12 months (eg a head of state or member of Parliament). EDD mitigates the risk that the proceeds of bribery and corruption may be laundered.
- A family member/known associate of a PEP.
- Any other situation that presents a higher risk of money laundering (eg having never met the client in person).

Test your ability to apply your knowledge of due diligence requirements to a realistic client-based scenario in **Practice example 6.5**.

Practice example 6.5

A solicitor is asked to complete a one-off transaction on behalf of a new client. The value of the transaction is £100,500. The client is based in England but is not near to the firm, so the solicitor and client have not met face to face. The transaction involves a party based in the Cayman Islands.

What CDD measures are likely to be appropriate in this case?

This is potentially a high-risk transaction. This is because the transaction involves a party based in a jurisdiction known to be a 'tax haven', the client has no discernible reason for selecting the firm and the solicitor has not met the client face to face. Because of this, it is highly likely that EDD will be appropriate.

Reporting requirements

It is important to understand that solicitors are expected to look out for signs of money laundering. The SRA has identified a number of 'warning signs' that solicitors should look out for. These are summarised below.

A *client* may display characteristics that could be a cause for concern. For example, a client may be secretive, uncooperative or evasive. The *client's behaviour* may also be a cause for concern. For example, where a client avoids personal contact, refuses to provide information or documentation or is known to associate with criminals. Solicitors often carry out transactions on behalf of clients. When doing this, solicitors should watch out for *unusual source(s) of funding.* For example, where there are very large cash deposits or deposits made from unknown third parties. Solicitors should also look out for *unusual transactions or instructions.* A solicitor's suspicions may be roused where a client insists that a transaction is completed urgently for no obvious reason or where a client instructs the solicitor to complete a loss-making transaction without a justifiable reason. A client's instructions may be regarded as unusual where a client has inexplicitly chosen the solicitor or firm to act for them (eg the client has chosen a firm not local to the client). Solicitors should be wary where there is *unnecessary movement of monies between different jurisdictions* or *movement of monies to/from jurisdictions known to be 'high risk'.*

Exam warning

In the SQE, watch out for these 'warning signs' in client-based scenarios. The inclusion of such signs may indicate that a solicitor is under an obligation to report suspicions of money laundering.

Where such warning signs alert a solicitor to possible money laundering, and the solicitor knows *or* suspects that a client is engaged in money laundering activity, they *must* report their concerns.

For the SQE, you must be able to identify:

- the appropriate person/body to receive reports
- the time for such reports to be made
- the procedure for making such reports.

The appropriate person/body to receive such reports

Where a solicitor *knows or suspects* money laundering activity, the solicitor *must* make a report to the firm's nominated officer/MLRO. The nominated officer/MLRO must then carefully consider the report and determine whether to make a SAR to the NCA. A SAR *must* be submitted to the NCA where the nominated officer *knows or suspects* money laundering activity.

When reports need to be made

Reports concerning money laundering must be made *as soon as is practicable*. Ideally, reports should be made before the relevant business takes place (eg before a suspicious transaction is completed). In some circumstances the solicitor may not know or suspect money laundering until the relevant business is underway or has concluded. To discharge their legal obligations, solicitors and nominated officers are required to make a report/disclosure as soon as is practicable once they suspect possible money laundering activity.

Procedure for making such reports

As noted in **Table 6.2**, firms are required to implement policies and procedures to deal with the risk of money laundering. These policies must be in writing and must outline the procedure to be followed when making a report to the nominated officer/MLRO. The firm *must* ensure that staff have access to this information and receive appropriate training on what to do should they need to make a report. The solicitor must make the report/disclosure to the nominated officer/MLRO.

Nominated officers/MLROs are responsible for submitting SARs to the NCA. The NCA encourages nominated officers to use the SARs' securely encrypted online system wherever possible. Alternatively, SARs can be submitted by post or fax. Where possible, a SAR should identify the suspect and give additional information about the suspect (eg address, account numbers, National Insurance Number), details of any other party/parties involved and a clear description of reasons for suspecting money laundering activity.

Failure to comply with reporting requirements

Solicitors and nominated officers who fail to report suspicion or knowledge of money laundering are likely to commit an offence under POCA.

THE PROCEEDS OF CRIME ACT 2002

The Proceeds of Crime Act 2002 (POCA) created a number of offences concerned with money laundering. It is part of the general law that applies to everyone (including solicitors). However, the Act also created a number of offences that only apply to those engaged in business in the regulated sector. For the SQE you are required to know the direct involvement and non-direct involvement offences under POCA. Direct involvement offences are those where the defendant is actually involved in the money laundering activity (eg a solicitor has transferred criminal property). Non-direct involvement offences deal with failure to respond appropriately to possible money laundering activity. The offences are summarised in **Table 6.3**.

Table 6.3: Non-direct involvement offences

Section	Overview of offence	Type of offence	Brief summary of offence
s 327	A solicitor commits an offence if he conceals, disguises, converts or transfers criminal property or removes it from the UK.	Direct involvement	Criminal property includes any direct or indirect benefit from criminal conduct. This offence is relevant to solicitors because solicitors will often 'transfer' or 'convert' property on behalf of clients.
s 328	A solicitor 'commits an offence if he enters into or becomes concerned in an arrangement which he knows or suspects facilitates … the acquisition, retention, use or control of criminal property by or on behalf of another person'.	Direct involvement	This offence is very broad and could cover any arrangement that assists in the process of money laundering by another person. To be guilty of such an offence, the defendant must 'know or suspect' that the arrangement facilitates money laundering.
s 329	A solicitor commits an offence if they acquire, use or have possession of criminal property.	Direct involvement	This provision is typically used to prosecute those who enjoyed the benefits of criminal conduct but did not engage in the criminal activity itself. It may, however, be relevant where a solicitor receives payment for work carried out for a client charged with a criminal offence and the payment is made from illegally acquired funds.

Table 6.3: Continued

Section	Overview of offence	Type of offence	Brief summary of offence
s 330	A solicitor commits an offence if they fail to disclose information about money laundering to the appropriate authorities. This provision is designed to ensure that information about suspected money laundering is passed to the relevant authorities promptly.	Non-direct involvement	To be guilty of this offence the solicitor must have known, suspected *or* have had 'reasonable grounds to know or suspect' money laundering. A solicitor may commit a s 330 offence even though they genuinely did not suspect that money laundering was occurring. The court will consider the information available to the solicitor at the time to determine whether the solicitor *ought to have known or suspected* that money laundering was occurring. The information *must* identify or assist in the identification of the money launderer or the whereabouts of the laundered property. Finally, the solicitor must fail to make a disclosure (report) to the firm's nominated officer as soon as practicable.
s 331	A nominated officer commits an offence if they fail to disclose information about money laundering to the appropriate authorities.	Non-direct involvement	Section 331 is similar to s 330, except it applies specifically to nominated officers/MLROs. Where, as a consequence of their role, a nominated officer knows or suspects, or has reasonable grounds to know or suspect, money laundering they *must* make the appropriate SAR to the NCA as soon as practicable. Failure to do so will constitute an offence under s 331.

Table 6.3: Continued

Section	Overview of offence	Type of offence	Brief summary of offence
s 333A There are two tipping-off offences under s 333A	Under s 333A(1) it is an offence to reveal to a third person that an internal or external disclosure/SAR has been made if such a revelation might prejudice an ensuing investigation. Section 333A(3) is very similar to s 333A(1) but applies where a third party is made aware of the fact that an investigation into a money laundering is being contemplated or carried out.	Non-direct involvement	Both tipping-off offences are concerned with circumstances where a solicitor alerts a suspect (or other third party) to the fact that a money laundering investigation is underway or is being contemplated. It is important to note that the solicitor need not *intentionally* frustrate an investigation. A solicitor will not commit a tipping-off offence where they did not know or suspect the disclosure would prejudice an investigation into money laundering. A solicitor will not commit a tipping off offence if an exception applies. For example, the disclosure is to a client and it is made for the purpose of dissuading the client from engaging in conduct amounting to an offence (s 333D(2)).

Now test your ability to apply your knowledge to a client-based scenario by answering **Practice example 6.6**.

Practice example 6.6

Just hours before a solicitor is due to carry out a transaction for a client, the solicitor discovers information that leads them to suspect that the transaction may be used for money laundering. The solicitor duly makes a report to a nominated officer, who subsequently submits a SAR to the NCA. The solicitor does not continue with the transaction because they are worried about breaking the law. Later that day, the client contacts the solicitor to ask why the transaction has not been completed. The solicitor, aware of their professional obligation to be honest, explains that they are unable to complete the transaction because they have reported concerns relating to possible money laundering.

Has the solicitor committed an offence under POCA?

While the solicitor has complied with their duty to report their concerns, it is likely that the solicitor has committed a 'tipping-off' offence under s 333A by informing the client that a report concerning money laundering has been made.

Exam warning

Solicitors owe clients a duty of confidentiality. This is professional conduct obligation. Naturally, a solicitor will have to breach this duty to make a report concerning suspected money laundering to the nominated officer or NCA. However, because such authorised disclosures are permitted by law, the solicitor will not breach their professional conduct obligations. The solicitor does not need the client's consent to disclose the client's information to the nominated officer or NCA. In fact, requesting such consent could 'tip off' a suspect and constitute an offence under s 333A. In the SQE, remember this exception to the duty of confidentiality. See ***Revise SQE: Ethics and Professional Conduct***.

Practical link

For the SQE FLK1 assessment, you need to remember that solicitors are expected to uphold high standards of ethics and comply with professional conduct obligations. A solicitor who commits an offence under POCA is also likely to face disciplinary proceedings.

Defences to money laundering offences

For the SQE FLK1 assessment, you need to know the defences to offences under POCA. **Table 6.4** provides an overview of the various defences to both direct and non-direct offences.

Table 6.4: Summary of defences

Defence	Brief overview	Offence(s)
Defence against money laundering (DAML), also known as the 'consent defence'	When submitting a SAR to the NCA, a nominated officer can request 'consent' for activities that would otherwise be prohibited under the POCA (eg continuing with a transaction that facilitates money laundering). Where the NCA grants such consent, the solicitor will have a DAML. The defence will only apply to activities that the NCA has specifically given consent for. If the NCA does not respond to the DAML request within seven days, the solicitor may assume they have 'deemed' consent. A solicitor will not have a DAML where the NCA refuses consent, but the solicitor carries out a prohibited act anyway.	s 327 s 328 s 329
Reasonable excuse defence	This defence applies where a solicitor/ nominated officer intended to make an authorised disclosure but had a 'reasonable excuse' for not doing so. There is no judicial guidance on what constitutes a reasonable excuse.	s 327 s 328 s 329 s 330 s 331
Adequate consideration defence	This defence only applies to s 329. It is available where a solicitor received adequate consideration (eg payment) for their services. It does not apply where the solicitor knew or suspected that their services may facilitate criminal activities. The defence would not apply where the payment for services is disproportionately higher than the value of the work undertaken.	s 329
Training defence	Firms are required to provide appropriate anti-money laundering training to their employees so that they can identify signs of money laundering. A firm's failure to provide such training may provide a solicitor with a defence. It does not apply where actual knowledge or suspicion existed.	s 330

Table 6.4: Continued

Defence	Brief overview	Offence(s)
Privileged circumstances	Privileged circumstances means information communicated: • by a client, or a representative of a client, in connection with the giving of legal advice to the client, • by a client, or by a representative of a client, seeking legal advice, or • by a person in connection with legal proceedings or contemplated legal proceedings. The exemption will not apply if information is communicated or given to the legal professional with the intention of furthering a criminal purpose.	s 330
Legal overseas conduct	This defence is applicable where the 'criminal' conduct occurred abroad and was lawful in the country where it took place, and had it occurred in the UK would not be punishable by 12 months' imprisonment or more.	s 330 s 331

Now try and answer **Practice example 6.7**.

Practice example 6.7

A solicitor is instructed to complete a transaction on behalf of a client. The solicitor has no prior business relationship with the client. The client transfers funds to the solicitor so that the transaction can be completed the following day. Hours before the transaction is due to take place, the client suddenly pulls out of the arrangement. The client requests that the solicitor returns the funds but asks that the money is paid via bank transfer into two overseas accounts. The solicitor suspects the client is engaged in money laundering so makes a disclosure to the firm's nominated officer.

Can the solicitor return the funds to the client as requested?

Returning the funds would likely constitute an offence under s 328 (becoming concerned in an arrangement that a person suspects facilitates the retention, use or control of the proceeds of crime). The solicitor would need to have obtained consent from the NCA in order to have a defence against money laundering.

KEY POINT CHECKLIST

This chapter has covered the following key knowledge points. You can use these to structure your revision, ensuring you recall the key details for each point, as covered in this chapter.

- The Equality Act 2010 defines nine protected characteristics and a range of prohibited conduct. A solicitor must not subject clients or prospective clients to conduct that is prohibited under the Act. Employers must not subject employees to conduct that is prohibited under the Act. Solicitors (in their capacity as service providers and/or employers) may also have to comply with positive duties under the Act.
- Money laundering enables criminals to benefit from their involvement in criminal activity. Anti-money laundering legislation is designed to hamper money laundering. Firms/solicitors must comply with the duties laid out in the MLRs.
- Firms *must* appoint a MLCO and a nominated officer (or MLRO) and solicitors must adhere to applicable CDD requirements.
- Once a solicitor knows or suspects that money laundering activity is occurring they *must* report their concerns to the nominated officer (or MLRO) as soon as is practicable. The nominated officer must then evaluate the report and, if appropriate, make a SAR to the NCA. SARs should be submitted as soon as is practicable. Failure to comply with these reporting duties is likely to constitute an offence under POCA.
- There are a range of direct involvement and non-direct involvement offences under POCA. There are also a number of defences available to these offences.

KEY TERMS AND CONCEPTS

- protected characteristics (**page 110**)
- prohibited conduct (**page 111**)
- money laundering (**page 118**)
- proceeds of crime (**page 119**)
- customer due diligence (CDD) (**page 120**)

SQE1-STYLE QUESTIONS

QUESTION 1

A solicitor working for a large law firm alleges that she has been subject to discriminatory treatment because of her religious beliefs.

Consequently, she commences a civil claim against the firm. A fellow colleague plans to give evidence against the employer. The employer becomes aware of the colleague's intention to give evidence against the firm. As a consequence of this, the colleague is informed that the firm will not consider his application for a promotion.

Has the employer engaged in any prohibited conduct under the Equality Act 2010?

A. Yes, the employer has subjected the colleague to harassment.
B. Yes, the employer has subjected the colleague to direct discrimination.
C. No, the employer is entitled to restrict access to promotions.
D. Yes, the employer has subjected the colleague to victimisation.
E. No, the employer's treatment of the colleague is not linked to a protected characteristic.

QUESTION 2

An employee with a disability at a firm of solicitors requests a parking space closer to the main entrance of the building. The employee's disability makes it difficult for the employee to walk unaided for long periods of time.

Which of the following best describes the employer's obligations to the disabled employee?

A. The Equality Act 2010 requires the employer to make any necessary adjustments to ensure that the employee with a disability is not placed at a disadvantage compared to those who do not have a disability.
B. The Equality Act 2010 requires the employer to make reasonable adjustments to ensure that the employee with a disability is not placed at any disadvantage compared to those who do not have a disability.
C. The Equality Act 2010 requires the employer to make reasonable adjustments to ensure that the employee with a disability is not placed at a substantial disadvantage compared to those who do not have a disability.
D. The Equality Act 2010 requires the employer to make significant adjustments to ensure that the employee with a disability is not

placed at a disadvantage compared to those who do not have a disability.

E. The Equality Act 2010 requires the employer to make adjustments to ensure that the employee with a disability is not placed at an unfair disadvantage compared to those who do not have a disability.

QUESTION 3

A solicitor acts for a client in relation to the acquisition of a company. Just hours before the transaction is due to complete, the solicitor acquires information that causes her to suspect her client will be using the transaction to launder money. The solicitor reports this to the nominated officer, who makes a SAR to the relevant authority.

What action should the solicitor now take?

A. Proceed with the transaction since the solicitor has made a disclosure to the nominated officer.

B. Proceed with the transaction only if she has obtained authorisation from the relevant authority.

C. Proceed with the transaction so that the client is not alerted to the money laundering disclosure and ensuing investigation.

D. Inform the client that she can no longer act on behalf of the client because a SAR is pending.

E. Inform the client that a disclosure has been made and then proceed with the transaction.

QUESTION 4

Some months ago, a newly qualified solicitor dealt with a transaction on behalf of a client. The client lives and works in the south-east of England. The firm is based in the north-east of England. The solicitor never met the client face to face. The transaction involved multiple jurisdictions. The solicitor failed to spot that the client was using the transaction to launder the proceeds of crime, despite the fact that the solicitor ought to have at least suspected that the client was involved in money laundering. The solicitor claims that she had not received any training on how to deal with suspected money laundering. The firm that employs the solicitor has no records to show the solicitor had undertaken the relevant training.

Which of the following statements most accurately outlines the solicitor's position in respect of liability under POCA?

A. The solicitor will most likely be liable for the offence of failing to make a disclosure.
B. The solicitor will most likely be liable for failing to make a SAR.
C. The solicitor will not be liable for an offence under POCA because she had no knowledge or suspicion of money laundering.
D. The solicitor has not committed an offence under POCA because it is the duty of the nominated officer to make SARs to the NCA.
E. The solicitor has likely committed a failure to disclose offence but is likely to be able to rely on the training defence.

QUESTION 5

A solicitor working for a law firm is approached by a prospective client. The client wants to establish a business relationship with the firm. The client needs advice and services in connection with divorce proceedings.

Which of the following best describes the solicitor's obligations in respect of CDD?

A. The solicitor may verify the client's identity applying the firm's standard CDD measures.
B. The solicitor must verify the client's identity applying simplified due diligence measures.
C. The solicitor must verify the client's identity applying EDD measures.
D. The solicitor will need to verify the client's identity if the solicitor suspects money laundering.
E. The solicitor must verify the client's identity applying the firm's standard CDD measures.

■ ANSWERS TO QUESTIONS

Answers to 'What do you know already?' questions at the start of the chapter

1) Direct discrimination involves the person being treated unfavourably because of a protected attribute, whereas indirect discrimination

occurs when a policy or rule applies to everyone but has the effect of disadvantaging someone because they have a protected characteristic.

2) The non-direct involvement offences under POCA are:
   - failure to disclose information (s 330)
   - failure to disclose (nominated officers) (s 331)
   - 'tipping off' (s 333A)
   - prejudicing an investigation (s 342).
3) False: solicitors are under a legal duty to report suspicions of money laundering to the relevant nominated officer.
4) The following defences are applicable to direct-involvement offences POCA:
   a. reasonable excuse defence
   b. overseas defence.
5) CDD refers to the measures taken to verify a client's identity before a solicitor establishes a business relationship with the client or undertakes occasional transactions on behalf of a client.

Answers to end-of-chapter SQE1-style questions

Question 1

The correct answer was D. The colleague's treatment is a consequence of the employer believing that the colleague will do a protected act rather than because of a protected characteristic. The relevant prohibited conduct is victimisation. Options A and B are incorrect because they identify the wrong prohibited conduct. Option C is incorrect because an employer cannot subject an employee to a detriment because they will or might do a protected act. Option E is wrong because victimisation does not need to be linked to a protected characteristic.

Question 2

The correct answer was C. An employer is obliged to make *reasonable* adjustments to prevent an employee with a disability suffering a *significant* disadvantage. The other options include incorrect descriptions of the obligation to make adjustments.

Question 3

The correct answer was B. The solicitor should only proceed with the transaction if they have received consent from the NCA. Without such consent, the solicitor commits a direct-involvement offence under POCA (options C and E are therefore incorrect). Option A is incorrect because a disclosure to the nominated officer does not provide a defence to money laundering. Option D is incorrect because the solicitor should not inform the client of the disclosure or proceed with the transaction.

Question 4

The correct answer was E. The solicitor was required to make a disclosure because she ought to have suspected money laundering (therefore option A is wrong). However, the firm's failure to provide training is likely to provide the solicitor with a defence. Option C is incorrect because it is sufficient to show that the solicitor *ought to have suspected* money laundering. Option B is incorrect because the offence related to failure to make a SAR applies to nominated officers only. Option D is incorrect because solicitors are required to disclose suspicion of money laundering to the nominated officer.

Question 5

The correct answer was E. Solicitors are obliged to apply due diligence measures before establishing a business relationship with a new client. The scenario does not suggest that there is a high risk of money laundering, so the solicitor does not need to apply EDD measures (therefore, option C is incorrect). Options A and D are incorrect because they suggest that the requirement for standard due diligence measures to be followed only applies in certain circumstances, which is incorrect. Option B is incorrect because simplified due diligence is not applicable to this type of case.

■ KEY CASES, RULES, STATUTES AND INSTRUMENTS

The SQE1 Assessment Specification does not require you to know any case names for the topic. However, candidates must know the Equality Act 2010 and the Proceeds of Crime Act 2002. You must be able to recall and cite these Acts in the SQE.

7

Financial services

MAKE SURE YOU KNOW

Solicitors deal with a wide range of legal matters. Occasionally, their work involves some sort of financial service or product. Such work tends to be incidental to the legal services that solicitors provide. Because they sometimes engage in certain financial activities, solicitors are subject to the same regulatory framework that applies to the financial services industry generally. The framework is designed to ensure that there is appropriate regulation and oversight of individuals and businesses offering financial services or products to consumers.

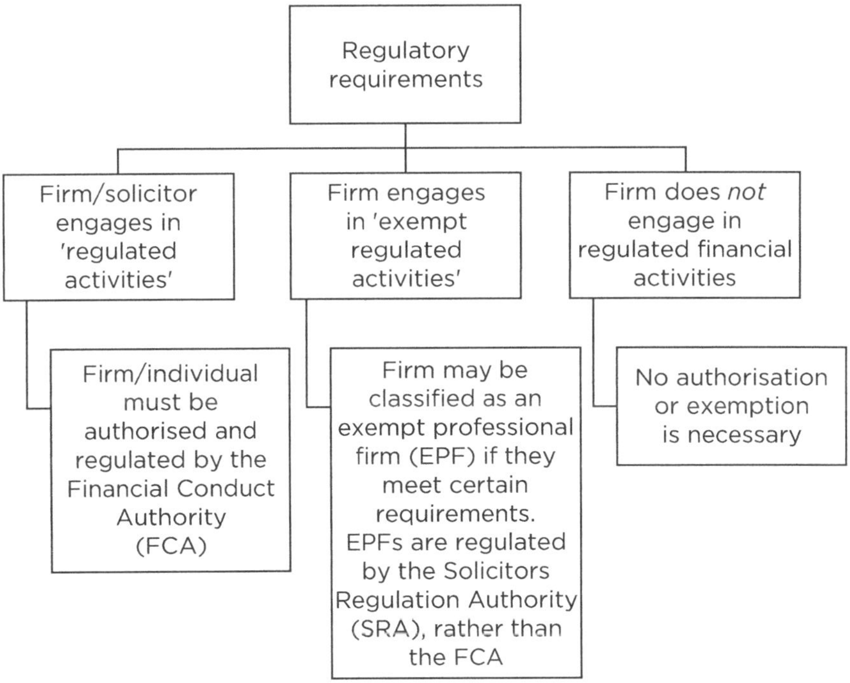

SQE ASSESSMENT ADVICE

For the SQE, you need to understand the relevant financial services regulatory framework and have an appreciation of its significance for solicitors. For SQE1, you are required to know the Financial Services and Markets Act 2000.

As you work through this chapter, remember to pay particular attention in your revision to:

- the relevance of the Financial Services and Markets Act 2000 and related secondary legislation to the work of a solicitor
- the financial services regulatory framework
- authorisation and how it applies to solicitors' firms
- the meaning of specified investments, specified activities and relevant exemptions.

WHAT DO YOU KNOW ALREADY?

Have a go at these questions before reading the chapter. If you find some difficult or cannot remember the answers, make a note to look more closely at that in your revision.

1) Which piece of secondary legislation sets out the 'regulated activities'?

   [The Financial Services and Markets Act 2000, page 139]

2) True or false: the term 'exempt regulated activities' refers to financial service activities that are not subject to regulation.

   [Designated professional body exemption, page 145]

3) Which regulatory body is responsible for regulating solicitors' firms relying on the designated professional body exemption?

   [The Financial Services and Markets Act 2000, page 139]

4) What does the term 'specified investment' refer to?

   [The Financial Services and Markets Act 2000, page 139]

5) Explain what is meant by the term 'the general prohibition'.

   [The general prohibition, page 139]

THE FINANCIAL SERVICES AND MARKETS ACT 2000

The primary piece of legislation dealing with the regulation of financial services is the Financial Services and Markets Act 2000 ('the Act'). The Act lays out the general framework for the regulation of financial services. It is important to note that many of the specific details of regulation are contained within pieces of secondary legislation. These are identified throughout the course of this chapter and are summarised in **Table 7.5** at the end of the chapter.

The general prohibition

To ensure that only appropriately qualified and skilled persons provide financial services to consumers, the Act contains a **general prohibition** that prevents businesses and individuals from carrying on certain **regulated activities** without appropriate authorisation.

> **Key term: general prohibition**
>
> The general prohibition is stated in s 19 of the Financial Services and Markets Act 2000. It provides that: 'No person may carry on a regulated activity in the UK unless authorised or exempt'. A person or business will commit a criminal offence if they breach the general prohibition.

A person will be classified as 'authorised' where they have obtained authorisation from the appropriate regulator. There are two financial regulators for the financial services industry, the Prudential Regulation Authority (PRA) and the Financial Conduct Authority (FCA). The PRA regulates financial institutions (like banks, building societies, etc). The FCA regulates businesses, firms and financial advisors. It is the FCA that is relevant to solicitors.

The Financial Conduct Authority

The FCA is guided by the statutory objectives set out in the Act. The FCA's strategic objective is to ensure that the relevant financial markets function effectively. Its operational objectives are:

- the consumer protection objective (ensuring an appropriate degree of protection for consumers of financial services)
- the integrity objective (protecting and enhancing the integrity of the financial system)
- the competition objective (promoting effective competition in the market).

Where the FCA has granted a person or firm authorisation to engage in regulated activities, that person/firm is subject to regulation by the FCA. The person will not breach the general prohibition if they have obtained FCA authorisation to carry on regulated activities.

Regulated activities

The general prohibition applies in respect of regulated activities. A person or business that engages in such activities must have authorisation from the FCA unless they are able to rely on an exemption (discussed later in this chapter).

Key term: regulated activities

In this context, the term 'regulated activities' refers to activities that can only be carried on by persons with appropriate authorisation or by persons exempt from such authorisation.

In essence, there are three components to a regulated activity, as shown in **Figure 7.1**.

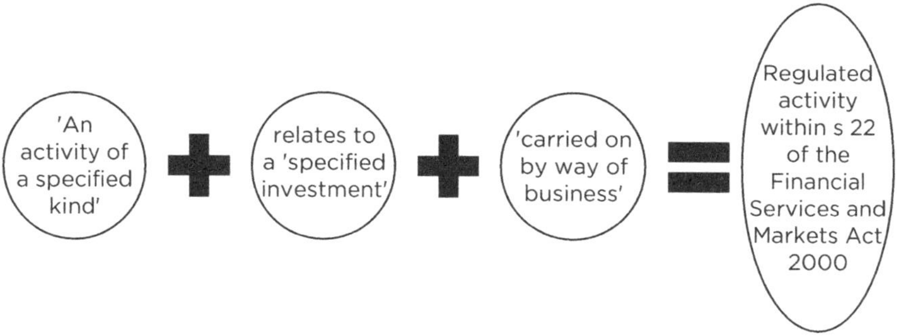

Figure 7.1: Components of a regulated activity

Put simply, *only* those activities that have been 'specified' in an order made by the Treasury are regulated activities, and such activities are only deemed to be regulated activities if they relate to certain types of investments (these are also specified by the Treasury) *and* are carried out in the course of business. The Treasury specifies the relevant activities and investments in the Financial Services and Markets Act 2000 (Regulated Activities Order) 2001 ('the Regulated Activities Order').

Specified activities

The full list of specified activities is extensive and is outside the scope of this guide, although **Table 7.1** gives some examples of the types of specified activities that are likely to be relevant to solicitors.

Table 7.1: Examples of specified activities

Activity	Brief overview
Dealing in investments as agent	A solicitor may 'deal as an agent' if they buy, sell, subscribe for or underwrite an investment on behalf of a client and commit that client to transactions.
Arranging deals in investments	Client transactions often involve investments. In such transactions a solicitor acts as a contact between the client and a third party. In such circumstances, a solicitor may be deemed to be 'arranging' deals in investments.
Managing investments	This relates to managing investments on behalf of a client. The solicitor must be actively involved in the management of the investment. Management must involve the exercise of discretion (it is not enough to simply hold investments on behalf of a client).
Advising on investments	Advising is where a solicitor gives *specific* advice on the merits of buying, selling, subscribing for or underwriting an investment.
Safeguarding and administering investments	This involves protecting and administering investments belonging to a client.

Exam warning

In the SQE, you may be presented with a realistic client-based scenario that involves a solicitor advising a client in respect of investments. Remember that a solicitor can give generic advice to a client without falling foul of the Act. Here, 'advising' on investments means giving *specific* advice to a client.

Specified investments

Specified investments are listed in Part III of the Regulated Activities Order. In the SQE, you may be asked to determine whether a particular activity is classified as a regulated activity. To make such a determination, you will need to be able to identify whether the activity relates to a specified investment. **Figure 7.2** (overleaf) provides some examples of the type of specified investments you should look out for.

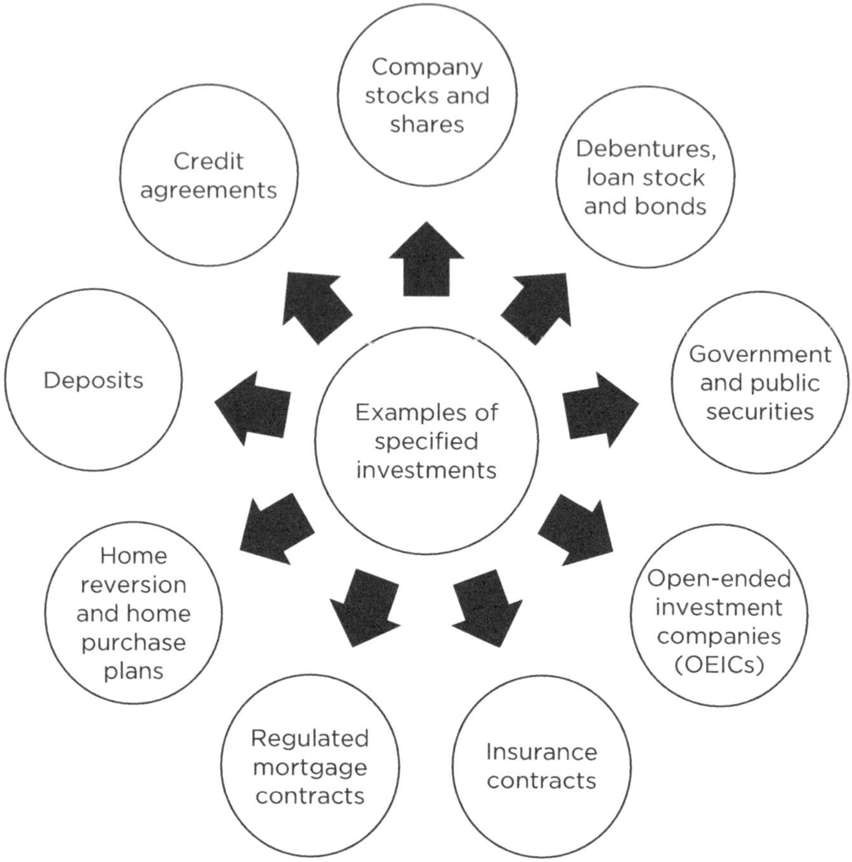

Figure 7.2: Types of specified investments

The Act states that the following investments will *not* be classified as specified investments:

- interests in land
- certain National Savings products.

Exam warning

In the SQE, watch out for specified activities that relate to investments in *land*. Such investments fall outside the scope of the Act. A solicitor who offers such advice may face disciplinary proceedings by the Solicitors Regulation Authority (SRA), but they will not commit an offence under the Act.

'Carried on by way of business'

Finally, for a specified activity to be deemed a regulated activity, the activity must be 'carried on by way of business'. For our purposes, this means that the solicitor must carry on the relevant activity in the course of the business (eg A solicitor, acting in that capacity, providing services to a client).

Revision tip

Remember that in order for the specified activity to be classified as a *regulated* activity, it *must* relate to a *specified investment.* For example, a solicitor who *advises* on an investment (this is the *specified activity*) must give advice that relates to a specified *investment* (eg one shown in **Figure 7.2**). Additionally, the activity (eg advising) must be carried on in the course of the solicitor's business (see **Practice example 7.1**).

Practice example 7.1

During the course of a meeting with a solicitor, a client asks the solicitor to advise on the merits of investing in a specific company by purchasing shares in that company. The solicitor offers the client advice.

Is such advice a regulated activity for the purposes of the Act?

Yes. The solicitor gives the advice in his capacity as the client's solicitor. Giving advice on the merits of a specific investment is a specified activity. Here, the advice relates to company shares. This is a specified investment. All three elements of the definition are satisfied. The activity will be classified as a regulated activity, unless an exclusion applies (discussed below).

Exclusions

The Regulated Activities Order also sets out a number of exclusions. Where an exclusion applies, an activity that would otherwise be a regulated activity is not regarded as such. **Table 7.2** (overleaf) provides an overview of the exclusions that are likely to be of particular relevance to solicitors.

Table 7.2: An overview of the exclusions

Exclusion	Overview	Applies to
Introducing an authorised person	This applies where a solicitor introduces a client to an authorised person but has no further role in arranging the investment.	Arranging
Arranging or dealing through an authorised third party (ATP)	This applies where an arrangement is based on the advice of an ATP or where the ATP deals with the investment. A solicitor cannot rely on the ATP exclusion if the solicitor receives any pecuniary reward (eg the solicitor is paid a commission) or other advantage for which the solicitor does not account to the client.	Dealing Arranging
Acting as a trustee, nominee or personal representative	This exclusion applies where a solicitor is acting as a trustee or a personal representative and does not receive additional renumeration for acting in that capacity.	Arranging Managing Safeguarding Advising
Activities carried on in the course of a professional or non-investment business	This exclusion applies where the activities that are carried out are deemed to be a necessary part of services provided by a profession or business that does not otherwise carry on regulated activities in the UK.	Dealing Arranging Advising Safeguarding
Activities carried on in connection with the sale of a body as a corporate	This exclusion applies where a transaction is to acquire or dispose of shares in a body corporate. It applies where the shares consist of or include 50% or more of the voting shares in the body corporate, and the parties to the acquisition are a body corporate, a partnership, a single individual or a group of connected individuals.	Dealing Arranging Advising

DESIGNATED PROFESSIONAL BODY EXEMPTION

As discussed above, individuals or businesses can obtain authorisation from the FCA directly. However, the Act also allows designated professional bodies to be exempt from such authorisation. In the SQE, you are expected to understand how the designated professional body (DPB) exemption applies to solicitors. The exemption can be relied on by firms that carry on certain regulated activities on an incidental basis (eg where the majority of the work the firm carries out is *not* regulated financial activity). If a firm is exempt, it is permitted to carry on certain types of regulated activities, known as **exempt regulated activities**. Where a firm carries on such activities, it will not breach the general prohibition.

Key term: exempt regulated activities

Exempt regulated activities are those activities that may be carried on by persons exempt from FCA authorisation by virtue of the designated professional body exemption of the Financial Services and Markets Act 2000.

The SRA, through the Law Society, is a DPB under the Act. This means that firms (including sole practices) authorised by the SRA may carry on exempt regulated activities without being regulated by the FCA if they can meet the conditions in s 327 of the Act. The relevant statutory conditions are outlined in **Table 7.3**.

Table 7.3: Relevant statutory conditions

Statutory condition	Brief explanation of condition
A person ('P') is a member of a profession, or controlled or managed by one or more such members.	A person must be classified as a member of a profession. Solicitors regulated by the SRA are deemed to be members of a profession.
P must not receive from a person other than his client any pecuniary reward or other advantage, for which he does not account to his client, arising out of his carrying on of any of the activities.	Solicitors must disclose to the client any payment or any other advantage they receive from a person (other than the client) for carrying on the regulated activity.

Table 7.3: Continued

Statutory condition	Brief explanation of condition
The manner of the provision by P of any service in the course of carrying on the activities must be incidental to the provision by him of professional services.	Financial services must not represent a major part of the firm's work. If they do, it will need FCA authorisation. In assessing whether the financial activities are 'incidental' to the firm's main work, consideration will be given to: • the scale of regulated activity undertaken • the extent to which exempt regulated activities are advertised as separate services (the greater the degree of separation between the professional services and the regulated activity, the less likely the activities will be considered as 'incidental' to the firm's main work) • the impression created by the way the firm provides regulated activities (eg does the firm specifically advertise the regulated activities?). Importantly, the regulated activity *must* arise from, *or be connected to*, a legal service provided to a client. This means a firm could not offer regulated financial services that are unconnected to a legal matter.
P must not carry on, or hold himself out as carrying on, a regulated activity other than (a) one that rules made as a result of s 332(3) allow him to carry on, or (b) one in relation to which he is an exempt person.	The activities that solicitors are permitted to carry out under the DPB exemption are laid out in the SRA Financial Services (Scope) Rules ('Scope Rules').
The activities must not be of a description, or relate to an investment of a description, specified in an order made by the Treasury for the purposes of this subsection.	The Treasury has laid out a list of activities that that cannot be provided by professional firms relying on the DPB exemption. They are stated in the Financial Services and Markets Act 2000 (Professions) (Non-Exempt Activities) Order 2001.

Table 7.3: Continued

Statutory condition	Brief explanation of condition
The activities must be the only regulated activities carried on by P (other than regulated activities in relation to which he is an exempt person).	Put simply, the exemption cannot be used by firms that are authorised and regulated by the FCA.

As noted in **Table 7.3**, the Scope Rules set out the exempt regulated activities that may be undertaken by exempt professional firms (EPFs). The SRA Financial Services (Conduct of Business) Rules ('the Conduct Rules') regulate the way in which EPFs carry on exempt regulated financial services activities.

The core regulatory requirements are detailed in **Table 7.4**.

Table 7.4: Core regulatory requirements

Rule 2: Status disclosure	This rule requires firms to disclose certain information about the 'status' of the firm. It must provide the information in writing before providing a service that includes the carrying on of a regulated financial services activity. The information should include: • a statement that the solicitor is not authorised by the FCA • the solicitor's name and practising address • the nature of the regulated financial services activities carried out by the solicitor • a statement that the firm is authorised and regulated by the SRA • a statement explaining that complaints and redress mechanisms are provided through the SRA and the Legal Ombudsman.
Rule 3: Execution of transfers	Where a solicitor has agreed or decided to effect a transaction, they must execute the transaction as soon as possible, unless they reasonably believe that it is in the client's best interests not to.
Rule 4: Records of transactions	Where a solicitor receives instructions from a client to effect a transaction, or makes a decision to effect a transaction, the solicitor must keep a record of the name of the client, the details of the instructions or the decision, and, in the case of instructions, the date on which they were received.

Table 7.4: Continued

Rule 5: Record of commissions	Where a solicitor receives a commission that is attributable to regulated financial services activities, the solicitor must keep a record of the amount of the commission and how the solicitor has accounted to the client.
Rule 6: Safekeeping of clients' investments	Where a solicitor undertakes the regulated financial services activity of safeguarding and administering investments, they must operate appropriate systems that provide for the safekeeping of assets entrusted to the solicitor by clients and others. Where such assets are passed to a third party, the solicitor should obtain an acknowledgement of receipt of the property; and if they have been passed to a third party on the client's instructions, the solicitor should obtain the instructions in writing.
Rule 7: Execution-only business	If a solicitor arranges to act for a client on an execution-only basis for any transaction involving a retail investment product (eg life policy), they must send the client written confirmation to the effect that: • the client had not sought and was not given any advice from the solicitor in connection with the transaction, or • the client was given advice from the solicitor in connection with that transaction but nevertheless persisted in wishing the transaction to be effected, • and in either case the transaction is effected on the client's explicit instructions.
Rule 8: Retention of records	All records should be retained for six years from the date the record was made.

Financial promotion prohibition

A solicitor who is not authorised by the FCA must be aware of the financial promotion prohibition. This is because s 21(1) of the Act states that a person 'must not in the course of business communicate an invitation or inducement to engage in investment activity'. Breach of the prohibition constitutes a criminal offence. The Financial Services and Markets Act 2000 (Financial Promotion) Order 2005 (SI 2005 No 1529) ('Financial Promotion Order') lists certain 'controlled' activities that may only be carried on by those with appropriate authorisation. It is important to note that EPFs cannot rely on the DPB exemption to communicate a financial promotion to a client in the course of business. However, EPFs may be able to rely on an exemption stated in the Financial Promotion Order.

Table 7.5: Key sources of information on financial services

Source of information	Overview
Financial Services and Markets Act 2000	Lays out the overarching regulatory framework
Financial Services and Markets Act 2000 (Regulated Activities) Order 2001, SI 2001/544	Specifies activities that are classified as 'regulated activities' for the purposes of the Act
Financial Services and Markets Act 2000 (Professions) (Non-Exempt Activities) Order 2001, SI 2001/1227	Specific activities that cannot be offered by EPFs under the DPB exemption
Financial Services and Markets Act 2000 (Financial Promotion) Order 2005, SI 2005/1529	Details the regulations concerning communication of financial promotions
SRA Financial Services (Scope) Rules 2001	Outlines the type of activities that can be offered by virtue of the DPB exemption
SRA Financial Services (Conduct of Business) Rules 2001	Outlines the way that exempt regulated activities may be offered by EPFs and solicitors
SRA website	Provides a range of useful information and guidance for solicitors and firms

■ KEY POINT CHECKLIST

- The Financial Services and Markets Act 2000 sets out the overarching regulatory framework for the provision of financial services.
- Certain financial service activities are classified as regulated activities under the Act.
- 'Regulated activities' can only be carried out by persons who are authorised by the FCA or persons who are exempt from authorisation.
- Activities are classified as 'regulated activities' where the activities are specified activities related to specified investments carried on in the course of business.
- The Regulated Activities Order also identifies some exclusions that may be relevant to solicitors. Where an exclusion applies, authorisation is not required.
- Most law firms rely on the DPB exemption. This exemption provides that certain professional bodies can regulate certain professions who carry on regulated activities on an incidental basis (eg it

is not their mainstream work). The exemption allows the SRA, through the Law Society, to regulate solicitors to carry on certain exempt activities.

- To be able to rely on the designated professional exemption, firms must comply with the conditions laid out in s 327 of the Act.
- EPFs must comply with the SRA Financial Services (Scope) Rules and the SRA Financial Services (Conduct of Business) Rules.

KEY TERMS AND CONCEPTS

- general prohibition (**page 139**)
- regulated activities (**page 140**)
- exempt regulated activities (**page 145**)

SQE1-STYLE QUESTIONS

QUESTION 1

A client instructs her solicitor to act for her in the purchase of 75% of the shares of a private limited company from another company. The solicitor is asked to arrange all of the necessary documentation for the purchase. Neither the solicitor nor her firm is authorised by the FCA to carry on a 'regulated activity'.

Will the solicitor breach the general prohibition if they carry out the activities for the client?

A. Yes, because the solicitor can only carry on a regulated activity if they have FCA authorisation.

B. No, because an exclusion applies where such a transaction involves at least 50% of the voting shares in the company.

C. No, because all law firms that are authorised to provide reserved legal activities through the SRA can rely on the DPB exemption.

D. No, because shares in a private limited company are not specified investments.

E. Yes, because no exclusions or exemptions apply.

QUESTION 2

A client asks a solicitor to explain the key differences between a repayment mortgage and an endowment mortgage. Neither the solicitor nor their firm is authorised by the FCA to carry on a regulated activity.

Can the solicitor give the explanation requested about the types of mortgages without breaching the general prohibition?

A. Yes, because the client has requested the advice from the solicitor.
B. No, because the advice is not a necessary part of the provision of his legal services.
C. Yes, because the solicitor is not receiving a fee in return for the advice.
D. Yes, because the provision of generic advice is outside the scope of the Financial Services and Markets Act 2000.
E. No, because the solicitor is not authorised by the FCA to give advice about mortgages.

QUESTION 3

A solicitor is contacted by an existing client and asked to give advice on whether she should buy a specific plot of land. The client plans to develop the land to return a profit. Neither the solicitor nor her firm is authorised by the FCA to carry on a 'regulated activity'.

Would the solicitor breach the general prohibition if they give the advice requested?

A. No, because the advice relates to investment in land, which is outside the scope of regulated activities.
B. No, because the client has requested the advice and the advice is incidental to the legal services provided to the client.
C. Yes, because the advice relates to a specified investment.
D. Yes, because the client is an existing client and the advice is incidental to the legal services provided.
E. No, because the advice is not specific.

QUESTION 4

A solicitor works for a firm that relies on the DPB exemption. The solicitor has acted for the client in a recent litigation matter. The client was awarded substantial damages. During a telephone conversation, the solicitor encourages the client to invest in shares in a company. The solicitor then provides the client with a brochure containing information regarding investing in a specific company.

Has the solicitor communicated a financial promotion in contravention of the Financial Services and Markets Act 2000?

A. No, the solicitor has provided legal advice to the client.
B. Yes, the solicitor has communicated a financial promotion and no exemptions are likely to apply.
C. No, because the advice was provided over the telephone and so an exemption will likely apply.
D. Yes, the solicitor committed an offence at the point they provided the written information to the client.
E. No, the solicitor works for an EPF so does not require FCA authorisation.

QUESTION 5

A solicitor introduces his client to a stockbroker. The solicitor does not give any advice relating to stocks to the client. The solicitor subsequently arranges for the client to buy some stocks in a company and completes all of the necessary paperwork on the client's behalf. The solicitor receives a fee of £100 for referring the client to the stockbroker. The solicitor decides to keep the fee but does not disclose this to the client.

Has the solicitor complied with the relevant SRA Financial Services (Conduct of Business) Rules 2001?

A. Yes, because the solicitor received a payment from someone other than the client.
B. No, the solicitor can rely on the introducing exemption.
C. Yes, because the solicitor has not charged the client the £100 fee.
D. No, the solicitor is entitled to receive financial benefits in exchange for such referrals.
E. No, the solicitor must disclose the referral fee to the client.

ANSWERS TO QUESTIONS

Answers to 'What do you know already?' questions at the start of the chapter

1) The Financial Services and Markets Act 2000 (Regulated Activities) Order 2001, SI 2001/544 lays out the regulated activities.

2) False: the term 'exempt regulated activities' refers to financial service activities that are regulated by a DPB (eg the SRA).
3) The SRA, on behalf of the Law Society, is the regulatory body responsible for regulating solicitors' firms relying on the DPB exemption.
4) The term 'specified investment' refers to the types of investments that are defined as such under the Financial Services and Markets Act 2000 (Regulated Activities) Order 2001, SI 2001/544.
5) Generally, solicitors not authorised by the FCA are not permitted to communicate a financial promotion to a client. They may only do so where an exemption applies.

Answers to end-of-chapter SQE1-style questions

Question 1:

The correct answer was B. There is an exemption where the investment relates to a body corporate and certain criterion are met (eg the transaction involves more than 50% of the shares). Option E is therefore incorrect. Option C is incorrect because only law firms that engage in exempt regulated activities may rely on the exemption and such firms must be registered. Option A is incorrect because some regulated activities can be carried on by virtue of the DPB exemption (and therefore FCA authorisation is not always required). Option D is incorrect because shares in a private limited company are specified investments.

Question 2:

The correct answer was D. The advice sought is generic and is therefore not caught by the Act. All other options are therefore incorrect because they refer to requirements linked to regulated activities.

Question 3:

The correct answer was A. Remember that land is not a specified investment (therefore, option C is incorrect). As such, activities relating to land investments are not caught by the Act. Because the advice does not relate to any regulated activities, options B and D are incorrect. Option E is incorrect because it refers to the nature of the advice given (the activity) rather than the nature of the investment (specified investment). It is worth noting that while the solicitor will not breach the general prohibition, they may face SRA disciplinary proceedings for giving such advice.

Question 4:

The correct answer was B. There is clear communication of a financial promotion. Such promotions cannot usually be communicated by those not authorised by the FCA (option E is incorrect). The solicitor is promoting an investment opportunity rather than providing legal advice (option A is therefore incorrect). No exemptions are likely to apply, so option C is incorrect. The communication first occurred over a telephone call (a real-time-communication), so option D is incorrect.

Question 5:

The correct answer was E. Under the SRA Conduct of Business Rules, solicitors are required to disclose such fees (eg referral fees) paid to the solicitor by a third party. Option D is incorrect because there is a requirement for the solicitor to disclose such fees to the client. Option C is incorrect because the fact the solicitor has not charged the client for the referral is irrelevant. Option A is incorrect because the solicitor did not disclose the referral fee to the client. Option B is incorrect because the 'introducing' exemption would not apply here as the solicitor received a fee, which was not disclosed to the client.

■ KEY CASES, RULES, STATUTES AND INSTRUMENTS

The SQE1 Assessment Specification requires that you must know the Financial Services and Markets Act 2000. The specification also states that you should be aware of relevant secondary legislation and source materials. As such, you are advised to familiarise yourself with the following instruments and rules:

- Financial Services and Markets Act 2000 (Regulated Activities) Order 2001, SI 2001/544
- Financial Services and Markets Act 2000 (Professions) (Non-Exempt Activities) Order 2001, SI 2001/1227
- Financial Services and Markets Act 2000 (Financial Promotion) Order 2005, SI 2005/1529
- SRA Financial Services (Scope) Rules 2001
- SRA Financial Services (Conduct of Business) Rules 2001.

8

Funding options for legal services

■ MAKE SURE YOU KNOW

Solicitors provide legal services to a diverse range of clients. Consequently, there are a range of funding options available to pay for legal services. For the SQE, you need to be aware of these funding options and be able to identify the type of funding that may be available or appropriate in realistic client-based scenarios.

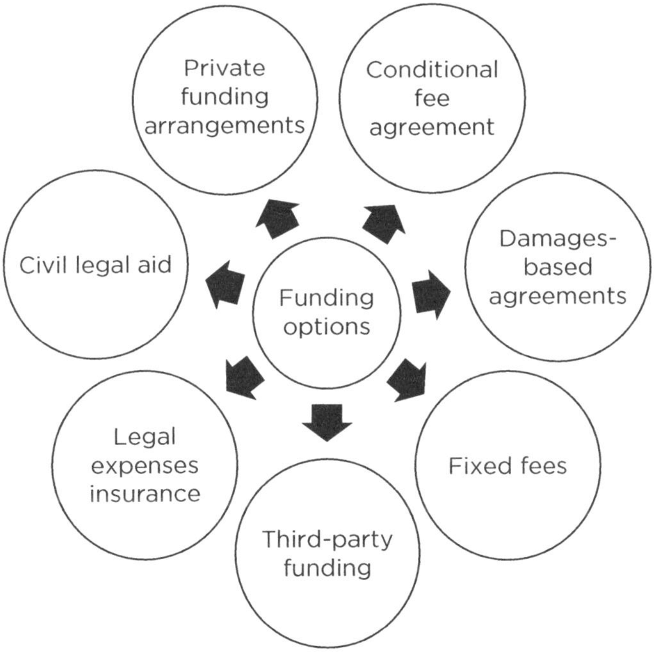

■ SQE ASSESSMENT ADVICE

As you work through this chapter, remember to pay particular attention in your revision to:

- private retainers
- conditional fee agreements
- damages-based agreements
- fixed fees
- third-party funding
- legal expenses insurance
- eligibility for civil legal aid.

■ WHAT DO YOU KNOW ALREADY?

Have a go at these questions before reading the chapter. If you find some difficult or cannot remember the answers, make a note to look more closely at that in your revision.

1) What is a 'conditional fee agreement'?

   [Conditional fee agreements, page 158]

2) What is a 'success fee'?

   [Conditional fee agreements, page 158]

3) True or false: legal aid is available to any person who does not have the means to pay for legal advice and/or representation.

   [Eligibility limits, page 166]

4) A home insurance policy provides cover for up to £6,000 of legal expenses. What type of legal expenses insurance is this an example of?

   [Legal expenses insurance, page 161]

5) True or false: conditional fee agreements and damages-based agreements typically cover all legal expenses incurred in civil cases.

   [Funding options, page 157]

FUNDING OPTIONS

For the SQE, you need to understand the range of funding options that may be used to pay for legal services. This chapter provides an overview of each funding option.

When a client engages the services of a solicitor, the solicitor should provide the client with a written **retainer** agreement setting out:

- the terms on which the solicitor will provide services to the client
- the work to be undertaken and completed
- how the work will be charged and paid for.

Key term: retainer

A retainer is the contractual agreement between a solicitor and a client.

An important aspect of a retainer is the agreed funding arrangement (eg how much the solicitor will charge the client and how such fees will be paid). These arrangements *must* be agreed at the outset and the terms must not contravene the Solicitors Regulation Authority (SRA) Rules and Standards.

Private funding arrangements

Private funding, as the name suggests, is where the client pays for the solicitor's fees themselves. The client is *personally* responsible for paying the costs. Costs are defined in the SRA Glossary as meaning the solicitor's fees and disbursements (eg other expenses, like the cost of instructing an expert witness). A solicitor's fees are calculated on the basis of the time spent on the client's case at a set hourly rate.

Key term: charging rate

The rate that a solicitor charges per hour is known as the solicitor's **charging rate**.

Different solicitors have different charging rates. Solicitors must, therefore, be transparent and upfront about their charging rate. Solicitors must also record the time spent working on a client's case. The precise method used for time recording varies from firm to firm, but the main principles are of universal application. Accurate time recording ensures that costs are correctly calculated. Typically, time is recorded in units (eg each unit is equivalent to six minutes of work). Solicitors record how many units of time they spend on the client's case. The amount of time a solicitor spends on a client's case varies depending on the nature and complexity of the matter. Common tasks undertaken by solicitors include preparation, drafting letters, making/receiving telephone calls, completing documents on behalf of the client and attending meetings/court. A solicitor will record the number of units (time) spent on such tasks. The units are then used to generate the client's costs (the client's 'bill', so to speak).

It is important to note that solicitors must *always* act in accordance with their overarching professional conduct obligations. The SRA Code of Conduct for Solicitors, Registered European Lawyers (RELs) and Registered Foreign Lawyers (RFLs) states that solicitors must provide their clients with accurate information about costs at the time of engagement and, as appropriate, as their matter progresses. Solicitors must also give an *estimated* overall cost for the matter. The final cost payable by the client is calculated on the basis of how much work the solicitor(s) actually completed. Therefore, the final sum payable may be more or less than the estimate. In this sense 'standard' private funding arrangements are 'open-ended'. However, a solicitor who deliberately overcharges a client will breach their professional conduct obligations and the overarching SRA Principles.

In some circumstances, a solicitor may agree to undertake work on a 'fixed-fee' basis.

Fixed fees

A solicitor may agree to complete work for a fixed fee. In such cases, the client is personally responsible for paying the solicitor's charges. These arrangements differ from the private funding arrangements discussed above because the final fee is fixed at the outset. This means the amount payable is agreed at the outset. Because the fee is fixed, it cannot be changed at a later date (unless the work transpires to be more expensive than the solicitor had anticipated *and* the client agrees to pay more).

Conditional fee agreements

A conditional fee agreement (CFA) is an agreement whereby the solicitor's fee is only payable in specified circumstances (the payment of the fee is *conditional*). The condition is that the client succeeds in their claim (or successfully defends a claim). To put it more simply, the client is usually only liable to pay the solicitor's fees if the client wins their case. You have probably come across these types of 'no win, no fee' agreements through TV/radio adverts. However, some CFAs require a client to pay lower fees, rather than no fees, in the event they lose their case.

A key point to note is that if fees are payable under a CFA, the client must pay the solicitor *more* than the solicitor would usually charge (more than their usual hourly rate). The fee payable is calculated on the basis of the solicitor's usual hourly rate *plus* a **success fee**.

Key term: success fee

A success fee is a charge payable by a client under a CFA. It is expressed as a percentage of the solicitor's usual hourly rate.

The success fee *cannot* exceed 100% of the solicitor's charging rate. The success fee should be set according to the risk associated with the case (eg a riskier case is likely to warrant a higher success fee and vice versa). When determining what success fee is appropriate, the solicitor should consider factors such as the likelihood of the client's case succeeding and the likely amount of damages that may be awarded. In personal injury cases, the success fee is capped at 25% of the general damages awarded (compensation awarded for pain, suffering and loss of amenity). So, if a client in a personal injury case is likely to recover £1,000 of general damages, the success fee is capped at £250. It is also important to note that the success fee is payable by the client. This means that if the client wins the case and the other party is required to pay their costs, the other party is *only* liable to pay the solicitor's usual hourly rate. *The client is liable for the success fee.* If the client loses, they do not have to pay their own solicitor's fees, but they may be liable to pay the other party's costs (including disbursements).

CFAs can be used in respect of any *civil* litigation matter except family proceedings. CFAs are only enforceable if certain statutory requirements are met. The CFA *must* be in writing and *must* state the success fee that will be payable (as a percentage). If the CFA does not satisfy these requirements and is deemed unenforceable, the client will not have to pay the solicitor's fees.

Exam warning

In the SQE, you may be required to determine whether a client is liable for (a) their own legal costs, (b) disbursements, (c) the other party's legal costs. Remember that CFAs typically *only* cover the client's own legal fees. If the client loses, they will not be liable for their legal fees, but they will most likely be liable for disbursements and for the other party's legal fees. This principle also applies in respect of damages-based agreements (DBAs), discussed below (see **Practice example 8.1**).

Practice example 8.1

A solicitor agrees to act for a client in a contract law matter. They agree a CFA with a success fee of 25%. The solicitor's usual charging rate is £100 per hour. The client's legal fees total £1,600, excluding the success fee and disbursements. The client wins the case. The other party is ordered to pay the client's costs (including disbursements).

What is the client's liability in respect of their solicitor's fees?

The solicitor's usual fees and disbursements will be paid by the other party. The client is liable to pay the success fee. In this case, the success fee is 25% of £100 per hour (£25 for each hour). The shortfall payable by the client is £400 (1,600/100 = 16 x £25).

Damages-based agreements

A damages-based agreement (DBA) is an agreement whereby a solicitor agrees to receive payment for their services *only* if the client is successful in their claim *and* the client obtains a financial benefit (eg damages). As the name suggests, in a DBA the solicitor's fee is linked to the level of damages awarded. For example, a DBA is set at 15%. If the client's case succeeds and the client is awarded £5,000 in damages, the solicitor would receive 15% of the £5,000 (£750). If the client's case was unsuccessful, the solicitor would not receive a fee. The client may, however, still be liable to pay the other party's costs (and may be liable for disbursements).

Even where a client's claim is successful and the other party is required to pay their costs, there may be a shortfall that the client will be liable to pay. In such circumstances, the costs paid by the other party will be deducted from the amount owed to the solicitor and the client will pay any shortfall from the damages awarded (see **Practice example 8.2**).

Practice example 8.2

A firm enters into a DBA with a client. The DBA is set at 10%. The client wins the case and is awarded £100,000 in damages. The other party is ordered to pay £9,000 towards the client's costs.
What is the client's liability in respect of their legal fees?

The DBA is set at 10% of the damages awarded. The client's case was successful, so the solicitor is entitled to 10% of the damages awarded (£100,000). The solicitor is therefore owed £10,000. The other party is liable to pay £9,000, which leaves the client with a shortfall of £1,000. This will be deducted from the damages and the client will receive £99,000.

DBAs must be capped at a maximum of 50% of the damages recovered by the client. The cap includes counsel's fees but no other disbursements. The client is, therefore, still liable for other disbursements. In personal injury cases, the cap is set at 25% of the damages awarded (excluding damages awarded for future financial loss). In employment cases, the cap is set at 35%.

In order for a DBA to be enforceable, it must comply with the relevant provisions of the Courts and Legal Services Act 1990 (CLSA). DBAs must be in writing, specify the proceedings to which the agreement relates and detail the payment arrangement, including when a fee is payable and why the DBA has been set at the level agreed. If the DBA does not satisfy these requirements and is deemed unenforceable, the client will not have to pay the solicitor's fees.

Legal expenses insurance

As has been outlined above, CFAs and DBAs do not cover the client's own disbursements and do not cover any liability the client has in respect of the opponent's costs. As such, it is often advisable for a client to take out legal expenses insurance. There are two types of insurance: before-the-event insurance (BTE) and after-the-event insurance (ATE).

Before-the-event insurance (BTE)

These are existing insurance policies that cover legal expenses. Cover is usually provided as part of an insurance policy, such as a car insurance policy or home insurance policy. It is also possible to get insurance policies specifically for the purpose of covering legal expenses. Insurance policies rarely cover all legal expenses in all legal proceedings. The scope and level of coverage will be specified in the insurance policy. Of course, the insurer must accept the claim. If the claim is accepted, the insurer is liable to pay the solicitor's fees, in line with the specific terms of the policy. It is common for the policy to cap the amount of legal expenses covered. In such cases, the client would be responsible for any shortfall.

After-the-event insurance (ATE)

ATE is taken out *after* the legal issue arises and covers legal expenses incurred in making or defending a case. ATE is available for most civil cases, except family proceedings. ATEs tend to cover the client's liability for their solicitor's fees, their opponent's legal fees and all disbursements. Because ATE tends to cover disbursements and the other party's legal fees, ATE is often used alongside CFAs and DBAs. ATE premiums can be expensive. The premium charged will be determined by the client's chances of success and the level of cover that is required. Of course, an insurer must be willing to provide cover for the matter in the first place. If a case has a low chance of success, a client may not be able to obtain ATE.

Third-party funding

As the name suggests, third-party funding arrangements are those where a third party, not connected to the proceedings, agrees to fund the cost of litigation. The funding usually covers the client's costs and disbursements, but the scope of the funding will depend on the precise terms of the agreement. The third party may be a union or organisation (eg a trade union) or a specialist litigation funding company. Most third-party funding is from litigation funding companies. Such companies cover the cost of litigation in exchange for a fee payable from the money the litigant receives when the case concludes. This type of funding tends to be used by commercial clients. The third party will only fund a case where the client has a good chance of success. After all, if the claim fails the third party will not be paid a fee!

LEGAL AID

Legal aid is available in criminal and civil cases, although the provision available for civil cases has reduced significantly over recent years. The scheme is administered by the Legal Aid Agency (LAA), and is governed by the Legal Aid, Sentencing and Punishment of Offenders Act 2012 (LAPSO). Firms must have a contract with the Legal Aid Agency to carry out legal aid work. It is important to note that your understanding of criminal legal aid is assessed as part of criminal practice, so this topic is not covered in this book. You may refer to ***Revise SQE: Criminal Practice,*** **Chapter 3** for a detailed overview of criminal legal aid.

Key term: legal aid

Legal aid is a scheme whereby eligible persons can have some or all of their legal expenses paid from public funds.

Civil legal aid

Civil legal aid is classified as either controlled work or licensed work. Licensed work is authorised by the LAA on a case-by-case basis. Solicitors usually determine a client's eligibility for funding for controlled work. Civil legal aid funding covers a range of legal assistance, outlined below.

Legal help

Legal help funding covers a solicitor giving basic advice to the client and undertaking a limited range of actions following that advice (eg drafting a letter). Legal help is controlled work.

Help at court

Help at court funding covers advice and assistance in respect of a particular court hearing. This includes advocacy work. Help at court is controlled work.

Legal representation

Legal representation is available to a client who is a party to proceedings or who is considering starting proceedings. It can cover dealing with the client's case and representing the client in the proceedings (if necessary). Legal representation is licensed work. Therefore, to receive legal representation funding the client must make an application to the LAA. If the client's application is successful, the LAA will issue a legal aid certificate. Civil legal aid is available in the following areas:

- some family law proceedings where the client is the victim of domestic abuse
- care proceedings
- cases where the client faces homelessness
- cases where the client has been subject to discrimination
- immigration cases.

Legal aid funding may also be approved on an 'exceptional' basis if the LAA believe that refusing the application would breach the client's human rights. Such cases are, naturally, uncommon.

Exam warning

In the SQE, you may be asked to assess whether a client is eligible for civil legal aid funding. Remember, the first step is to establish whether the case is one where civil legal aid is available. Make sure you are familiar with the types of cases where such funding is available. Candidates often make the mistake of focusing *only* on the client's financial circumstances.

It is not enough to show that the type of case is one where civil legal aid may be available. The client *must* also demonstrate that they are eligible for such funding. Eligibility is assessed on the basis of the merits of the case and the client's financial circumstances.

Merits test

In all cases, the LAA will assess:

- the prospects of success
- cost-benefit.

The merits test to be applied will depend on the type of legal assistance required and the type of case. These are outlined in **Table 8.1**.

Table 8.1: Merits test applicable in civil legal aid work

Type of work	Applicable merit test
Legal help, help at court	Subject to the 'sufficient benefit test'. Legal aid will only be available if there is a sufficient benefit to the client, having regard to the circumstances of the case, including the client's personal circumstances.
Legal representation	Legal representation is dependent on the client's prospects of success. Generally speaking, funding will be refused where the prospects of success are assessed at less than 50%. Where the client's case involves money (eg a claim for damages), consideration will be given to the amount of damages that are likely to be covered against the likely costs involved in the case. Where the case does not involve money, consideration must be given as to whether the benefits to be gained justify the likely cost of pursuing the case. This is assessed by evaluating whether a 'reasonable client' would pursue the case if they were privately funding the matter. In either case, the LAA may also refuse funding if they believe that alternative sources of funding are available to the client (eg a CFA).

Means test

Even if a client is able to satisfy the 'merits test', they may still not be eligible for legal aid funding. A client will only be eligible for legal aid where their capital and income is below £8,000 (£3,000 for immigration cases). The client must produce an accurate and full account of their financial circumstances so that their 'means' can be properly assessed. The assessment also takes into account the income and capital of the client's partner (if they have one).

Where the client receives any relevant welfare benefit, they automatically qualify for legal aid. The relevant welfare benefits are:

- universal credit
- income support
- income-based job seeker's allowance
- income-related employment and support allowance
- guarantee credit element of pension credit.

Eligibility limits

Where the client is not in receipt of any of the benefits outlined above, the *income test* calculates the client's gross income. If the client's gross monthly income exceeds £2,657 the client does not qualify for legal aid. If the client's gross monthly income is £2,657 or less the assessment will calculate the client's disposable income. This is achieved by deducting living costs, etc. The client will only qualify for legal aid if their monthly disposable income is less than £733. It is important to note that even if the client satisfies the means test, they may still be required to contribute something towards their legal fees.

Revision tip

You can check the relevant eligibility limits on the government's website.

Criminal legal aid

Criminal legal aid is available to cover the cost of a defendant's legal representation. While criminal legal aid is more widely available than civil legal aid, there are eligibility requirements that *must* be satisfied. You need to be familiar with such requirements for SQE. Because criminal legal aid is assessed as part of criminal practice on SQE1, you should refer to ***Revise SQE: Criminal Practice*** for information about criminal legal aid.

Summary

Remember that, for the SQE, you need to know all the funding options covered in this chapter. **Table 8.2** provides a useful revision aid to help you revise the various funding options available.

Table 8.2: Key revision points for funding

Funding arrangement	Key revision points
Private funding arrangement	The client pays for the work completed. Charges are calculated according to the solicitor's charging rate.
Fixed fees	The client pays a predetermined fixed (set) fee for the work completed.

Table 8.2: Continued

Funding arrangement	Key revision points
Conditional fee agreement (CFA)	A CFA is an arrangement whereby the solicitor's fee is only payable in specified circumstances. If the client is successful, the solicitor receives their legal fees plus a success fee. If the client is unsuccessful, the solicitor receives no fee at all (or receives a reduced fee).
Damages-based agreement (DBA)	If the client is successful, the solicitor receives a percentage of the damages received. If the client loses, the solicitor receives no fee.
Before-the-event insurance (BTE)	The solicitor's fees are covered by an existing policy. The solicitor's fees are paid by the relevant insurer.
After-the-event insurance (ATE)	An insurance policy is taken out to cover the client's legal fees, disbursements and the client's liability for the opponent's costs in the event the client loses the case.
Third-party funding	A third party provides funding for litigation, usually in exchange for a fee payable from money the client is awarded.
Legal aid	Legal aid is a scheme that allows eligible persons to have some or all of their legal expenses paid in prescribed circumstances. It is available in both civil and criminal cases (but note that distinct eligibility requirements apply).

■ KEY POINT CHECKLIST

- There are a range of funding options available to pay for legal services:
  - private funding arrangement
  - fixed-fee private funding arrangement
  - conditional fee agreement (CFA)
  - damages-based agreement (DBA)
  - before-the-event insurance (BTE)
  - after-the-event insurance (ATE)
  - third-party funding
  - legal aid.
- It is important to note that CFAs and DBAs do not typically provide cover for disbursements or the other party's legal fees.

- In a CFA the success fee cannot exceed 100% of the solicitor's usual charging rate.
- In a DBA the maximum fee payable is 50% of the damages awarded.
- Legal aid is a scheme that allows certain individuals to have their legal fees paid from public funds. Legal aid is available in criminal and civil cases. A client must satisfy the relevant eligibility requirements to qualify for legal aid.

KEY TERMS AND CONCEPTS

- retainer **(page 157)**
- charging rate (**page 157**)
- success fee (**page 159**)
- legal aid (**page 163**)

SQE1-STYLE QUESTIONS

QUESTION 1

A solicitor agrees to act for a client on a 'no win, no fee' CFA. The success fee is set at 20%. The solicitor's usual charging rate is £200. The client's claim is successful. The client is awarded £2,500 in damages. The solicitor's fees amount to £2,000.

What success fee will the client be liable to pay?

A. A sum of £500 payable from the damages awarded.

B. A sum of £400.

C. A sum of £2,000.

D. A sum of £2,400.

E. The client is not liable to pay a success fee.

QUESTION 2

A firm enters into a damages-based agreement (DBA) with a client in an employment law matter. The DBA is recorded in writing, signed by the client and set at 40%. The client wins the case and is awarded substantial damages.

Which of the following statements most accurately describes the status of the DBA?

A. The DBA is unenforceable because DBAs cannot be used in employment law matters.
B. The DBA is enforceable because the client's case was successful.
C. The DBA is enforceable because it is in writing.
D. The DBA is enforceable because it is in writing and signed by the client.
E. The DBA is unenforceable because it is set too high.

QUESTION 3

A client instructs their solicitor to act on their behalf in relation to divorce proceedings. The client has very limited financial resources and is in receipt of welfare benefits. The client only needs assistance filling out the relevant court documentation.

Is the client eligible for legal aid?

A. Yes, the client passes the means test because she is in receipt of welfare benefits.
B. No, the client passes the means test but legal aid is not generally available for divorce proceedings.
C. Yes, the client only requires basic help to complete court documents.
D. Yes, the client satisfies the interests of justice test and the means test.
E. No, the client would need to satisfy the full means test to be eligible for legal aid.

QUESTION 4

A client is bringing a personal injury claim against a hotel owner for an injury suffered whilst on holiday. The client intends to pay all of their legal costs through an existing travel insurance policy they purchase on an annual basis.

What type of funding is the client using to fund the personal injury claim?

A. After-the-event insurance.

B. Conditional fee agreement.

C. Third party funding.

D. Before-the-event insurance.

E. Damages-based agreement.

QUESTION 5

A client instructs a solicitor to act in respect of an employment law matter. The solicitor agrees to act on a damages-based agreement (DBA). The DBA is set at 30%. The client loses the case and is ordered to pay the other party's costs.

Which of the following best describes the client's liability in respect of his legal expenses?

A. The client is liable to pay the other party's costs. This can be taken from the damages awarded.

B. The client does not need to pay the other party's costs because under a DBA the client is not liable to pay legal fees if they lose the case.

C. The client is liable for their own legal fees and the other party's costs.

D. The client is liable to pay for the other party's cost, but this will be paid by the firm because the client's case was unsuccessful.

E. The client is liable to pay the other party's fees.

■ ANSWERS TO QUESTIONS

Answers to 'What do you know already?' questions at the start of the chapter

1) A CFA is an arrangement whereby a solicitor's legal fees are only payable in specified circumstances.

2) A success fee is a charge payable by a client under a CFA.
3) False: although legal aid is available in both civil and criminal matters, it is subject to strict eligibility requirements. It is not, therefore, available to any person who is unable to pay for advice or representation.
4) This is an example of a BTE insurance policy.
5) False: CFAs and damages-based agreements do *not* typically cover disbursements or liability in respect of another party's costs.

Answers to end-of-chapter SQE1-style questions

Question 1:

The correct answer was B. The success fee is set at 20% of the solicitor's usual fees. The solicitor's usual hourly fee is £200 so the success fee is £400. Option A is incorrect because success fees are not linked to the damages awarded. Options D and E are wrong because they include the solicitor's usual fees. The claimant was successful so they are liable to pay the success fee (therefore option E is incorrect).

Question 2:

The correct answer was E. DBAs can be used in employment law cases (so option A is incorrect), but in such cases the relevant cap is 35%. In this case, the DBA was set at 40%, which exceeds the 35% cap. Options B, C and D are all incorrect because they fail to acknowledge that the DBA is set above the relevant cap and is therefore unenforceable.

Question 3:

The correct answer was B. While the client is in receipt of a relevant benefit, legal aid is not available in divorce proceedings, unless the client is the victim of domestic abuse (option A is therefore incorrect). Options C and D are incorrect because the case is not one where legal aid is available. Option E is incorrect as the full means test is relevant to criminal proceedings only.

Question 4:

The correct answer was D. The client intends to fund the litigation through an existing travel insurance policy. Such policies often include insurance cover for legal expenses, although the degree of cover provided varies significantly from policy to policy. If a client funds litigation through an *existing* insurance policy that includes some form of cover for legal expenses, they are using before-the-event insurance. This is a form of legal expenses insurance. All other options are incorrect.

Question 5:

The correct answer was E. Under a DBA, if a client loses the case they are not liable to pay their legal fees (option C is therefore incorrect). The client is personally liable to pay the other party's costs if they lose. The client's liability is not impacted by the DBA (options B and D are therefore wrong). Option A is incorrect as the client is personally liable for the costs.

■ KEY CASES, RULES, STATUTES AND INSTRUMENTS

The SQE1 Assessment Specification does not require you to know any case names, or statutory materials, for this topic. You are, however, expected to be familiar with the legal principles and rules outlined in the chapter.

Index